Great Breeders and Their Methods

Samuel Riddle, Walter Jeffords and the
Dynasty of Man o' War

by Rommy Faversham

The Russell Meerdink Company, Ltd.
Neenah, Wisconsin 54956 U.S.A.

Cover design & layout by Bosetti Production Art & Design

Library of Congress Cataloging-in-Publication Data

Faversham, Jerome L.
  Great breeders and their methods : Samuel Riddle, Walter Jeffords,
  and the dynasty of Man o' War / by Rommy Faversham.
    p. cm.
  Includes bibliographical references and index.
  ISBN-13: 978-0-929346-77-9 (hardcover : alk. paper)
  1. Riddle, Samuel Doyle, 1861-1951. 2. Jeffords, Walter Morrison,
  1883-1960. 3. Horse breeders--United States--Biography. 4. Man o'
  War (Race horse) 5. Thoroughbred horse--Breeding--United States
  --History. 6. Thoroughbred horse--United States--Pedigrees--History.
  7. Horse trading--United States--History.   I. Title.
  SF336.R52F38 2005
  636.1'082'0922--dc22
  [B]

2005022247

Published by

The Russell Meerdink Company, Ltd.

1555 South Park Avenue, Neenah, Wisconsin 54956
USA
(920) 725-0955
www.horseinfo.com

Printed in the United States of America

TABLE OF CONTENTS

CHAPTER ONE

The Franchise

"When a great man appears we are naturally afraid of him and extraordinarily jealous and envious. We honor him, if at all, when he is safely dead, and pick poor sticks from among our contemporaries to set in high places.

But horses are another matter, and we honor them when they deserve it. None has ever deserved it more than Man o' War."

~ *The New York Sun, June 1920*

Judging from the eyewitness accounts, the charts, a mountain of poetry and prose, even modern polls and ratings, Man o' War continues to be the most celebrated racehorse in American history. Never has an individual established himself to be so far superior to his contemporaries as did this great creature.

Unlike most of America's greatest champions who typically carry the racing colors of their breeders, Man o' War passed through the auction ring as a raw prospect. The change in ownership was the beginning of a new racing and breeding dynasty. To presume that Samuel D. Riddle, whose high bid secured the providential yearling, was just the odd beneficiary of freakish luck would be to neglect the details that led to this most fortuitous of turf investments. As legendary baseball executive Branch Rickey later pointed out, "luck is, quite often, the residue of design." The long and storied fortunes of Riddle and his close partner, Walter M. Jeffords, are testament to this.

Sam Riddle's life spanned a remarkable segment of American history, beginning with a nation struggling for survival and ending with its emergence as the world's greatest power. When Riddle entered racing in the 1880s it was still, for the most part, a novel sport. By the time of his passing, it had become a major international industry.

Not apparent to most pundits is the alliance between Riddle and his business partner Walter Jeffords. The alliance was guided by a series of strategies to be described in the following chapters. The cooperative efforts of these two men allowed them to hold sway in the most prestigious of East Coast racing venues.

Never in American racing has one horse accounted for so much of the success ultimately achieved by its masters. Of the 127 stakes winners bred by the two stables, 112 carried the blood of Man o' War. Man o' War was, for them, a Promethean flame, the ultimate franchise player.

By the same token, most of the breed-shaping influence Man o' War has had on the contemporary Thoroughbred can be traced to the designed matings of Riddle and Jeffords. Their legacies have been solidly and permanently linked. Riddle and Jeffords are responsible for a remarkable number of Thoroughbred matings that have shaped key male and female strains of the modern American runner. Their efforts led to many of the genetic pathways that now connect the 19th and 21st century versions of the breed.

The Man o' War empire, with its legendary headquarters at Faraway Farm outside of Lexington, Kentucky, is a fascinating historic enterprise to dissect and analyze.

The vibrant times corresponding to Man o' War's youth ushered in a golden age in American racing made more glamorous by the great chestnut's impact on the sport.

This unrivaled attention seemed to ignite a series of mischaracterizations, particularly in regard to Riddle, by several noted writers and historians. One of the more peculiar aspects of the Riddle saga is the negative light in which he has often been described in the annals of racing and breeding, including his portrayal in the hit movie *Seabiscuit*. What caused Samuel Riddle to become the most maligned owner-breeder in American turf history? This surely wasn't "the residue of design." These misperceptions have congealed over time into a myth – one that is worth debunking.

Even though the pedigrees depicted in this book are of racehorses who lived decades earlier, the successful inbreeding patterns they demonstrate serve as useful models in the configuration of contemporary matings as well.

As with other successful franchises, the accomplishments of Samuel Riddle and Walter Jeffords demonstrate what is possible when high-end talent meets capital equipped with solid design.

CHAPTER TWO

THE PLAYERS

*"There wasn't any story. He just kept on
winning. There were no reverses in his life.
Nothing of heartbreak, of setbacks or real
conflict – All the things which make for
drama and suspense!"*

*Film director Dave Butler
turning down a Warner Brothers offer
to make a Man o' War biography*

The Man o' War saga begins with the birth of Samuel Doyle
Riddle in Glen Riddle, Pennsylvania, on July 1, 1861, only weeks after
the first volleyed shots of the American Civil War. He was the eldest son
of Samuel Riddle and his second wife, Lydia C. Doyle, of Chester,
Pennsylvania.

Riddle's father arrived in Philadelphia in 1823, an immigrant
from Belfast, Ireland, with only five Spanish dollars and a sea chest that
he carried on his back. After finding work at several different cotton mills,
the adroit Riddle soon began his own cotton yarn spinning operation. The
business prospered.

In 1842 the elder Riddle purchased a large parcel of land in
Delaware County, Pennsylvania, about 16 miles west of Philadelphia.
He named the property Glen Riddle in honor of the homeland of
his ancestral family, the Riddells of Glen Riddells in the lowlands of
Scotland. The Riddells' ancient Scottish manor, dubbed Friars Carse,
is where 18th century poet Robert Burns wrote some of his best-
known works.

Over the next 30 years, Glen Riddle grew to more than 6,000 acres with five large textile mills, more than 200 dwellings, a town with post office, and 5,000 employees. Business boomed, particularly in the early 1860s when the Glen Riddle mills received large government contracts to supply the Union Army with material for uniforms and blankets.

Good fortune at Glen Riddle granted young Samuel Doyle Riddle all the advantages of a country squire. His love of horses began at an early age. He grew up around elaborate stables and paddocks where blooded horses were a tradition. Riddle would later claim that he was lifted onto his first horse "sometime during the War Between the States." He became a fine judge of horses of all categories and was a student of breeding and training.

Samuel D. Riddle was educated at Pennsylvania Military College and graduated in 1879. He then went on to Swarthmore College where he became a classmate and close friend of John Howard Lewis, one of the nation's top amateur riders who later became one of the most accomplished steeplechase trainers of his era.

After leaving Swarthmore, Samuel D. Riddle joined his older half-brother, Henry, in their father's many enterprises, including the Samuel Riddle, Son & Company in Philadelphia.

Riddle married Elizabeth Dobson in 1883, the daughter of another wealthy Philadelphia-area textile manufacturer. Like her husband, Mrs. Riddle was known for her style and candor.

Years after Man o' War had become a legend, Riddle made an undiplomatic remark to friends, with his wife present, suggesting the day he acquired Man o' War was the greatest day of his life.

"Sam, the greatest day of your life was the day you married me," Mrs. Riddle shot back.

Considering the many accounts that credit Elizabeth Riddle with rousing her husband to buy the future super star at his sale, her quip would appear to have been particularly well founded.

Riddle eventually became the president of the Riddle Company but his number one passion was always the sporting world. Growing up in the heart of the Pennsylvania fox hunting country, Riddle developed an interest in fox hunting and steeplechase racing. He established his own pack of fox hounds, known as "Mr. Riddle's Hounds." The pack descended from the hounds General Lafayette presented to General Washington after the Revolutionary War. Riddle bred them not only for their speed and conformation, but also for their unique "music." The Riddle Hounds were a source of special pride for the huntsmen of the Rose Tree Hunt Club, the oldest hunt club in the U.S. The father of John Howard Lewis was one of its founders. Riddle eventually served as the club's president.

Following the path of other sportsmen from that era, Riddle progressed from hunters to steeplechasers, and eventually to flat racing. His first important racehorse was Swarthmore, which John Howard Lewis raised from a mare bred by President Ulysses S. Grant. Although he raced in the colors of the famed equine artist Henry Stull, Swarthmore was actually owned by Riddle and Lewis. The two named him in honor of their alma mater.

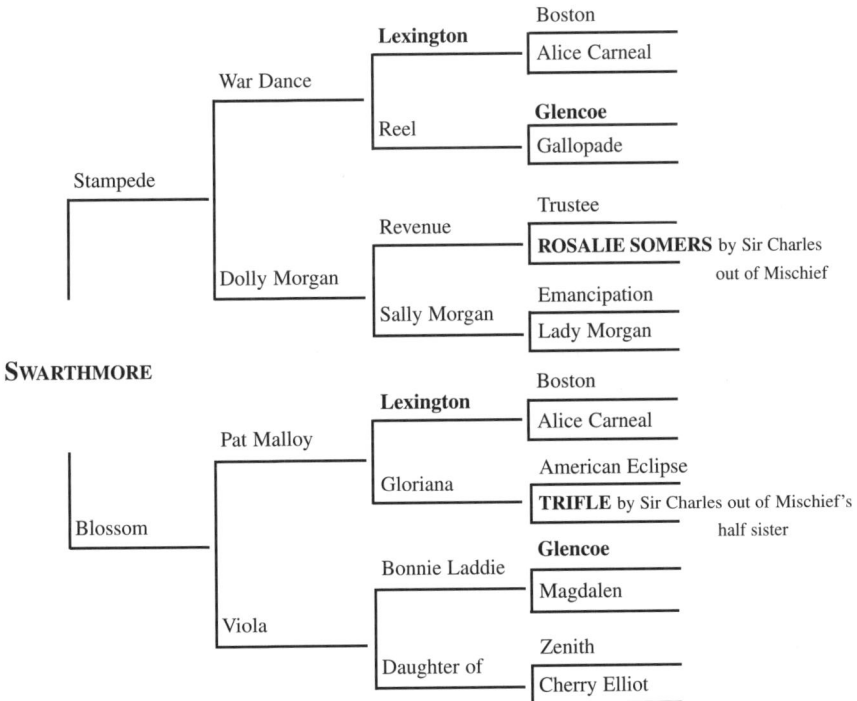

```
                                                    Boston
                                   Lexington
                                                    Alice Carneal
                    War Dance
                                                    Glencoe
                                   Reel
                                                    Gallopade
      Stampede
                                                    Trustee
                                   Revenue
                                                    ROSALIE SOMERS by Sir Charles
                    Dolly Morgan                                      out of Mischief
                                                    Emancipation
                                   Sally Morgan
                                                    Lady Morgan
SWARTHMORE
                                                    Boston
                                   Lexington
                                                    Alice Carneal
                    Pat Malloy
                                                    American Eclipse
                                   Gloriana
                                                    TRIFLE by Sir Charles out of Mischief's
      Blossom                                                         half sister
                                                    Glencoe
                                   Bonnie Laddie
                                                    Magdalen
                    Viola
                                                    Zenith
                                   Daughter of
                                                    Cherry Elliot
```

Swarthmore etched his name into the racing annals when he captured the 1887 Kenner Stakes at Saratoga, a valuable test for three-year-olds. According to one of Lewis' obituaries in *The Thoroughbred Record*, Swarthmore went off at exceptionally long odds that day and Messrs. Lewis, Riddle and Stull made what was described as a "killing."

Swarthmore has an interesting pedigree, one that served as a harbinger of the kinds of inbreeding patterns that would appear decades later when Riddle was making his mark as a breeder.

Like many American Thoroughbreds of the late 19th century, Swarthmore was closely inbred to the great stallions Lexington and Glencoe. More distinct, however, was the 4x4 cross of Rosalie Somers and her three-quarters sister Trifle, both outstanding racemares and producers during the 1830s and 40s. Both Revenue, broodmare sire of Swarthmore's sire (Stampede), and Pat Malloy, Swarthmore's broodmare sire, were from the same family.

Several years earlier, Bob Miles was an important multiple stakes winner at Saratoga. He was sired by Pat Malloy out of Dolly Morgan (Stampede's dam), thus demonstrating this very rare cross in reverse. The mating of sires and dams with ancestors from the same family, as in this case, would become a key strategy for the Riddle camp in years to come.

Riddle won the Kenner Stakes again 33 years later in 1920 with Man o' War (when it was called the Miller Stakes) and twice more with that one's sons War Glory and War Relic, in 1933 and 1941. Four times over 54 years!

During the 1890s, Riddle did not own any major stakes winners, but he did have several useful runners, including Passmore and Sea Bird who ran at the Gloucester track in New Jersey.

Early in the 1900s, Riddle campaigned a trio of his hunt horses in show jumping competitions where they were said to have never been beaten. One of these, Major Treat, later became Man o' War's closest companion. He served as a calming influence for the fiery colt through-out his two seasons at the track, sometimes accompanying him all the way to the post.

Back home in Delaware County, Riddle's favorite watering hole was Baron Dougherty's Hotel and Bar in nearby Leiperville. The bar attracted a colorful mix of factory workers, prize fighters and wealthy sportsmen. One of the waiters working there in 1917 was Jack Dempsey. Two years later he became world heavyweight champion, a title he held for seven years. In a boxing ring set up behind Dougherty's, Dempsey trained and sparred his way to boxing immortality. Over the years, Riddle enjoyed the fight exhibitions staged there, some featuring other great names from the sport.

The Riddles never had children, but they developed a close relationship with Mrs. Riddle's niece, the former Sarah Dobson Fiske and her husband, Walter Jeffords. The Jeffords lived at Glen Riddle near their uncle and aunt at the estate they called "Hunting Hill." Jeffords shared Sam Riddle's love of the turf and the two soon became close business partners.

Walter Morrison Jeffords was born in Philadelphia on August 8, 1883. His family had ties to the horse business having originally settled in Lexington at the start of the 19th century. His grandfather Alexander Brand bred Thoroughbreds at Glengarry Farm near Lexington.

Jeffords, after graduating from Yale University, entered his family's pottery business and later demonstrated success on his own in a number of business ventures. During World War I, he was commissioned an Ensign in the Naval Reserve Flying Corps. After discharge from the service, the sleek and bright Jeffords became a valuable ally for Riddle and shared in the treasures of Man o' War's best blood.

By 1915, Riddle, now in his mid-50s, was a sharply dressed, mustachioed fellow, usually described in aristocratic terms as having the manner of an English general resembling a Roman senator. He owned a successful business, enjoyed a high social standing with the hunt club set and had many friends and family. He wanted more.

Riddle enjoyed the camaraderie of Thoroughbred turfdom's great families – the Whitneys, Wideners, Belmonts – without being quite one of them. To be an equal in this social circle he needed the "big" horse.

The first step Riddle took in his quest for the "big" horse was to build a first-class training center. He purchased a sprawling farm that once encompassed 17,000 acres in Worcester County on Maryland's Eastern Shore near the town of Berlin. Riddle chose this region in the belief that the salt air breezes and bluegrass of Worcester would be particularly favorable for the wintering of his racing stable. Riddle built a one-mile oval and spacious yellow barns with green roofs that provided shelter for 60 horses. Holly Grove Road, a dusty lane across from the farm, led to a nearby Pennsylvania Railroad siding where the horses arrived and departed on specially outfitted railcars. He named his new, state-of-the-art facility Glen Riddle Farm.

Main training barn at Glen Riddle Farm in Maryland as it looked before the farm became the site of an upscale residential development.

Stalls form a single row down the center
of the barn, opening on both sides and
surrounded by a jogging or walking track.

Stall interior

Riders and grooms' quarters

When the Riddles came to visit they stayed in the farm's white colonial frame house built in 1869. It featured eight master bedrooms and seven baths. The rooms were furnished and decorated with antique Hepplewhite and Sheraton furniture, rare leather-bound books, paintings and ship models. There was also a six-car garage and a dormitory for 25 riders.

The main residence at Glen Riddle was destroyed by fire in 1969.

The farm also accommodated Riddle's love for fox and raccoon hunting. The vast property had marvelous little creeks and lagoons for fishing, another of its master's favorite pastimes. The Riddles soon earned a reputation for giving lavish afternoon garden parties that featured the perfect mint julep.

Glen Riddle Farm enjoyed almost immediate success at the track. In 1916, Yankee Witch, the first runner to carry her barn's new colors, captured a pair of important stakes. She won the Rosedale Stakes at the Jamaica course on Long Island as well as the prestigious Spinaway Stakes at Saratoga where she beat year-end divisional champion Koh-I-Noor. Riddle privately purchased the two-year-old daughter of *Ogden from John E. Madden. Yankee Witch was the first of several successful runner and broodmare prospects Riddle would purchase from Madden, who had already established himself as one of the top breeders and horse traders of his day.

Riddle's black silks with yellow sash and sleeve hoops would soon be among the most highly recognized in American turf history.

The circumstances leading to Riddle's acquisition of Man o' War began in the spring of 1917 when the United States entered the Great World War.

The call to arms was a national appeal that America's most powerful horseman, August Belmont II, could not ignore. The 65-year-old placed all of his racing interests on hold and offered his services to his country.

One of the leading owner-breeders of his era, Belmont was chairman of both The Jockey Club and the New York Racing Commission. These two organizations ruled American racing with an iron hand. Belmont II was seen as a benevolent but dominant leader of the two organizations.

Belmont was responsible for development of the innovative New York subway plan, the Interborough Rapid Transit Company (IRT). This company soon merged with the above-ground transportation activities of fellow business mogul and horseman William Collins Whitney.

Combining their efforts, Whitney and Belmont revitalized racing at Saratoga Springs and then shifted their focus to the construction of a new track on Long Island. Belmont Park, named after the late August Belmont I, opened in 1905. The elder Belmont was a major benefactor to the redevelopment of horse racing after the Civil War, later becoming a successful owner-breeder in his own right. The inaugural season of the new track featured the Belmont Stakes, also named after August I, which was transferred to the new facility from Morris Park. Decades later, this contest would become the final jewel in the Triple Crown – the last and longest in a trio of classic races for three-year-olds.

August Belmont II invested heavily in his idea to build an eight-mile canal across Cape Cod. The canal would shorten the shipping routes between Boston and New York by 75 miles and avoid dangerous waters. Unfortunately, the project proved far more costly than original estimates and sapped Belmont of his financial resources. The project would prove to be a success years after his death.

The Belmonts' sense of national duty in time of war began with August I, a German immigrant, who held ties to the Rothschild banks of Europe. Belmont reached New York in 1837. His rapid accumulation of wealth and power made him able to personally organize and fund an entire Union regiment during the Civil War.

When the U.S. entered World War I, August II sought and received a commission as major in the Quartermaster Corps. He served in France and Spain where he was placed in charge of securing and training horses for service in the military overseas.

By late 1917, changes in Belmont's priorities led to significant cutbacks in his breeding and racing operations. As a result, valuable employees were let go and valuable horseflesh was sold.

Louis Feustel grew up in the Belmont organization. By his mid-20s, Feustel had become one of Belmont's primary conditioners. With the cutbacks, however, he was now available to train for someone new. Riddle quickly availed himself of the opportunity, seeing the young Feustel as having the kind of background and experience he was seeking.

Feustel began working at Belmont's stable at the age of 10. He galloped Man o' War's ill-tempered grandsire Hastings and was foreman during the period when Man o' War's sire, Fair Play, was at the farm. In 1910, he became a head trainer for Belmont. Three years later, Feustel trained his first champion, Rock View (by Rock Sand out of Fair Play's full sister Golden View). Rock View was top three-year-old colt, winning a number of important engagements including the Travers Stakes. Soon thereafter, Feustel was winning big races with Belmont's handicap star Stromboli (by Fair Play) – the Metropolitan H., Suburban H., etc. Few horsemen had the knowledge and experience of the Fair Play line that Feustel enjoyed.

Louis Feustel and August Belmont II in 1924. Feustal grew up in the Belmont organization. Through his experience with Man o' War's grandsire, Hastings, and sire, Fair Play, as well as training many of Fair Play's runners, he recognized the potential of Man o' War.

Absorbed with the war effort and financially drained by the Cape Cod project, Belmont decided to part with most of his 1918 yearling crop. A series of package deals to privately sell off the 21 individuals failed. As a result, the lot was shipped from his Nursery Stud outside of Lexington to Saratoga Springs for the annual summer yearling sale. All of the yearlings were already named, probably by Mrs. Belmont, and most had names with military themes.

Exactly who from the Riddle camp was primarily responsible for recognizing Man o' War as a superior auction prospect is in doubt. With such a prize for one's ego, there was no shortage of those seeking credit. In the years to come, whenever it was brought up, Riddle claimed the honor was his. After his patron's death, Feustel contradicted his former boss' story. In his version, it was his own sharp eye that picked out the future phenomenon with an assist from Mrs. Riddle who appealed to her husband to buy the colt with the remark, "Louie likes him, and he's the one who's got to train him . . ." From other sources, it is claimed that James K. Maddux, an avid sportsman from Warrenton, Virginia, and one of Riddle's best friends, was integral in selecting Man o' War.

Perhaps the potential was recognized by all of them. Belmont later claimed that he considered keeping the Fair Play-Mahubah colt for himself but resisted, fearing that potential bidders would view his other yearlings as mere culls.

As a yearling, Man o' War was a tall and gangly individual with the high head carriage typical of the Fair Plays. He had a rounded star and faint stripe on his face, which was slightly Roman in profile. Due to Belmont's reluctance to put him in the sale, Red was not prepared like the other yearlings who were fat and glossy.

It was said to be Riddle's belief that the copper chestnut could be made into a fine show jumper if he did not do well on the flat. But there was also a special look about him for those who could see it. Later on, noted turf writer Joe Palmer would refer to it as "a look of eagles."

What is known for sure is that on Saturday, August 17, 1918, at the Fasig-Tipton Saratoga Yearling Sale, Riddle made what has been described as the best investment in turf history when his proxy bid of $5,000 landed the young Man o' War.

The actual bidding on Man o' War was performed by the Riddles' friend Ed Buhler, whose business was supplying much of Manhattan with manhole covers. More remarkably, Buhler was the uncle of renowned equine artist Richard Stone Reeves. The artist credits his own passion for the turf to seeing Man o' War's son War Admiral win the Belmont Stakes in 1937.

Sam Riddle's use of a trusted agent like Buhler to buy Man o' War at the lowest possible price made good sense. In the previous few summers Riddle made a reputation for himself by spending large sums of money on Saratoga yearlings. Now, armed with Louis Feustel as his trainer-adviser, he had come to shop the first-ever Belmont consignment.

If ever there was a time to play one's cards close to the vest, it was then. In all, Sam Riddle spent $28,000 for 11 yearlings that summer. Only one turned out to have any talent.

The underbidder for Man o' War is said to have been Mrs. Robert L. Gerry. As the story goes, she was dissuaded from bidding higher by her husband whose feeling was "that's too much for a horse!"

Others attending the sale were said to have mixed feelings about Man o' War. Some felt he was too tall and awkward to make a good runner. Others pointed to the colt's nervousness and his questionable female line.

The 1918 Saratoga yearling sale averaged $1,107 with six colts fetching more than the $5,000 Riddle paid for Man o' War. Belmont's Nursery Stud consignment of 21 individuals brought a total of $54,450, far more than what the Major had sought privately.

The highest-priced yearling at the spa sale was Switch, a French-bred son of Sweeper II, winner of the Two Thousand Guineas in England. The compact, powerful-looking colt was purchased for $15,600

A compact, powerful colt, Golden Broom was owned by Mrs. Walter Jeffords and trained with Man o' War at Glen Riddle. The bright chestnut colt is shown here with trainer Mike Daly and jockey E. Ambrose.

(a Saratoga record) by Mrs. Walter Jeffords who would re-christen him Golden Broom. The bright chestnut colt with four white feet was bred by Herman Duryea, a close friend of Harry Payne Whitney, son of the previously noted W.C. Whitney. When his father died in 1904, H.P. Whitney acquired much of his father's best stock at the dispersal sale and then carried on the family legacy, becoming one of the premiere owner - breeders of the American Turf.

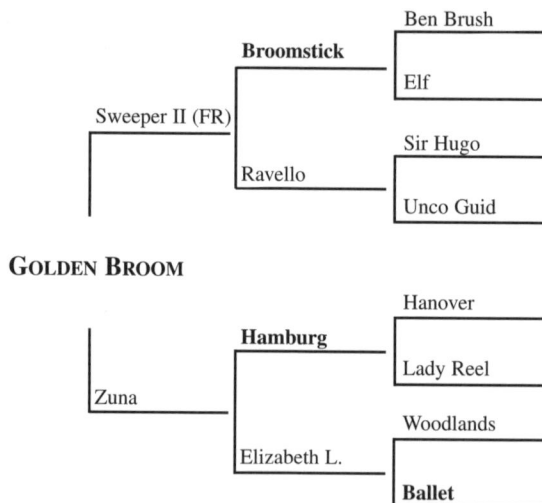

```
                                            Ben Brush
                          Broomstick
                                            Elf
          Sweeper II (FR)
                                            Sir Hugo
                          Ravello
                                            Unco Guid
GOLDEN BROOM
                                            Hanover
                          Hamburg
                                            Lady Reel
          Zuna
                                            Woodlands
                          Elizabeth L.
                                            Ballet
```

Besides Golden Broom's fine conformation, the Jeffords, as well as the other bidders, must have been impressed by his Whitney-crafted pedigree. It was remarkably similar to that of the best filly H.P. Whitney ever bred: Regret.

In 1915, Regret became the first filly to win the Kentucky Derby, an occasion that seemed to bring a whole new level of respect to the race. She was an undefeated champion at two and three and faced both sexes. Regret was later inducted into Racing's Hall of Fame. In 1915 her younger full brother Thunderer also won the prestigious Futurity Stakes at Belmont.

Interestingly, Regret, her grandsire Ben Brush, as well as the sire of her second dam, Riley, all descended from the same American family (Family A1).

In 1915, Regret became the first filly to win the Kentucky Derby. Her pedigree and that of her full brother Thunderer shared many similarities with that of Golden Broom.

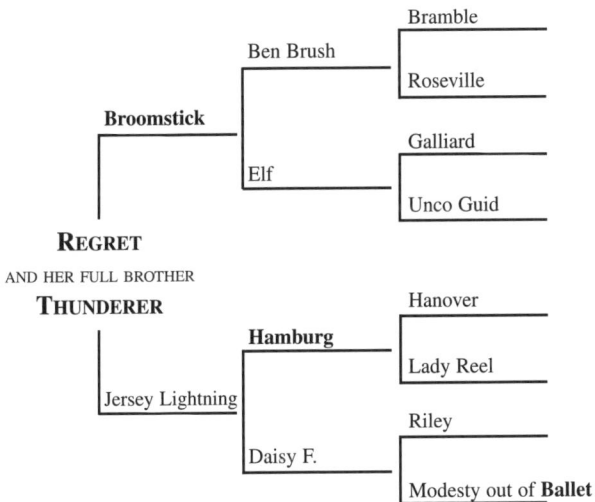

```
                                               ┌─ Bramble
                              ┌─ Ben Brush ─────┤
                              │                 └─ Roseville
              Broomstick ─────┤
                              │                 ┌─ Galliard
                              └─ Elf ───────────┤
                                                └─ Unco Guid
      REGRET
AND HER FULL BROTHER
     THUNDERER                                  ┌─ Hanover
                              ┌─ Hamburg ───────┤
                              │                 └─ Lady Reel
              Jersey Lightning┤
                              │                 ┌─ Riley
                              └─ Daisy F. ──────┤
                                                └─ Modesty out of Ballet
```

23

The close relations Golden Broom shared with Regret and Thunderer made his pedigree a fashionable one for the 1918 sale and the Jeffords paid accordingly. They were already familiar with this family, having campaigned Golden Broom's French-bred half brother Red Sox, by Irish Lad, who broke his maiden at Saratoga the previous year.

The Riddles' Man o' War and the Jeffords' Golden Broom were broken soon after their purchase. Man o' War and Golden Broom, along with the other yearlings acquired by the two families over the course of the season, were then shipped to Glen Riddle Farm on the Maryland shore for the winter.

Jeffords and Riddle had developed adjoining training centers at Glen Riddle. There, Man o' War, Golden Broom and their peers were walked and ridden, rubbed and washed.

Occasionally, the yearlings would sprint an eighth or a quarter mile, under wraps. It was in these light contests that Man o' War proved himself to be the most promising yearling on the Riddle side of the farm, as his long and powerful stride was beginning to reveal itself.

The Riddle and Jeffords camps, while training and racing under separate colors, were always closely associated. One of their customs was to give the yearlings their first real trials in sets of two, one from each farm. Man o' War was matched against Golden Broom who, as expected, had emerged as the year's favorite from among the Jeffords string. The two are said to have been tested at one, two and then three furlongs with the Riddle charge slower into stride, never getting on even terms with Golden Broom in any of their three encounters.

So much for first impressions.

A special notice was given to the colt by the stable boys who started calling him "Big Red" or just "Red" – which is how he has been referred to ever since. As one magazine article later put it, "only strangers address him as Man o' War."

After the trials, Big Red went into winter quarters with nothing more in the way of speed to be asked of him for the duration of the cold weather. Eating became his main job and the voracious appetite he demonstrated then and throughout his amazing career would help account for his great strength and rugged good health.

Riddle's 10-year-old big brown hunter, Major Treat, served as one of the training ponies at Glen Riddle. Almost immediately, Red and the Major struck up a close friendship that had a calming effect on the excitable young colt. For the Feustel barn, Major Treat was the perfect natural tranquilizer for the hot-blooded chestnut. His role in the Man o' War saga appears to have been immeasurable.

By the end of winter, and to no one's surprise, Red had filled out into a handsome two-year-old, deep-chested and with muscles that made his coat ripple. In early spring training at Glen Riddle, he started showing his followers that he still liked to run as much as he liked to eat.

Riddle was now spending most of his time supervising the training of the two-year-olds. By this point, Thoroughbreds had become his life's absorbing interest and to create even more time for his horses, he entrusted his nephew-in-law Jeffords with his famous American fox hound pack and the continuation of their line.

In May 1919, the Riddle and Jeffords strings were shipped to Havre de Grace, a long bygone Maryland racetrack built on bluffs overlooking the mouth of the Susquehanna River. For Man o' War, it was the beginning of a two-year campaign that brought new vitality to the sport and reestablished the limits a horse was capable of reaching.

A chronicle of all of the details throughout Man o' War's racing career is beyond the scope of this book. The first truly comprehensive account of his life, *Man o' War* by Page Cooper and Roger L. Treat, was published in 1950 (which means it could have been one of the last books Riddle had an opportunity to read before he died the following year). It is a wonderfully written book with a thick appendix that will satisfy the most ardent of "Red" fans. Fifty years later, in 2000, Edward L. Bowen's *Man o' War* was released, providing another valuable narration that added new and interesting stories and angles. A third in-depth volume on the life of Man o' War, *Chained Lightning*, is anticipated soon from racing historian and Saratoga Springs denizen Dorothy Ours.

Man o' War's juvenile campaign consisted of 10 races, nine of them stakes events at distances ranging from five to six furlongs.

A sign of his lasting greatness is that so much more has been made of his lone defeat than all nine of his victories that year, most of which came in effortless fashion. Big Red's only defeat took place on August 13th at Saratoga in the Sanford Memorial. On that day, just about everything that could go wrong for a racehorse, in fact, did. Even though it sullied his otherwise perfect record, the effort was illustrative in showing how many different negative things had to occur to get this wonder-colt beat.

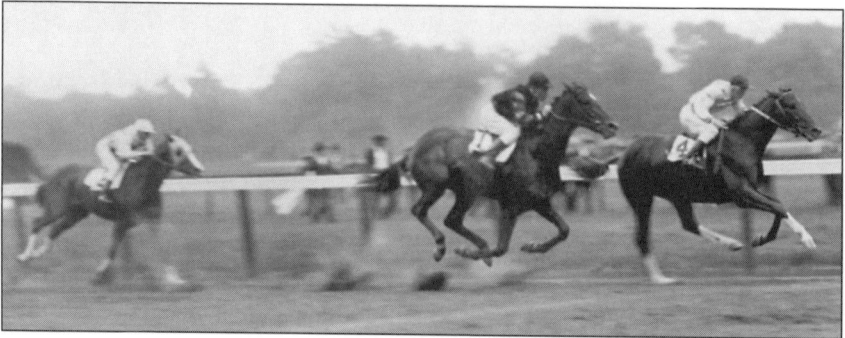

UPSET reaches the finish ahead of MAN o' WAR in the Sanford Stakes, GOLDEN BROOM third.

SANFORD MEMORIAL STAKES. Saratoga, Aug. 13, 1919. 3-4 Mile. Allowances. Guaranteed value, $5,000. 2-year-olds. Net value to winner, $3,925; second, $700; third, $300.

Index Horses	Eq't A	Wt	PP	St	$\frac{1}{4}$	$\frac{1}{2}$	Str	Fin	Jockeys	Owners	O	H	C	P	S
UPSET	w	115	5	1	2^h	2^1	1^h	$1\frac{1}{2}$	KnappW	H P Whitney	10	12	8	7-5	1-3
MAN O' WAR	w	130	6	5	4^4	$3^{11}/_2$	3^3	2^3	LoftusJ	Glen Riddle F	7-10	4-5	11-20	out	out
GOLDEN BROOM	wb	130	3	2	$1\frac{1}{2}$	1^1	$2^{11}/_2$	3^2	AmbroseE	Mrs W Jeffords	9-5	$2\frac{1}{2}$	$2\frac{1}{2}$	1-2	out
†CAPT. ALCOCK	wb	112	4	7	7	7	6^2	$4^{11}/_2$	RobinsonCJ	E Madden	50	200	100	30	10
ARMISTICE	wb	112	2	3	5^3	5^2	$5\frac{1}{2}$	5^5	McAteeL	W R Coe	50	50	50	15	5
DONNACONA	w	112	7	4	3^1	4^5	$4\frac{1}{2}$	6^1	KelsayW	G W Loft	20	50	30	8	3
THE SWIMMER	wb	115	1	6	6^3	$6^{11}/_2$	7	7	SimpsonR	T F Henry	30	50	50	15	5

†Added starter.   Time, :23^1/5, :46^4/5, 1:11^1/5. Track fast.

Winner–Ch. c, by Whiskbroom II.–Pankhurst, by Voter, trained by James Rowe; bred by Mr. Harry Payne Whitney.

Start poor and slow. Won driving; second and third the same. UPSET followed the leader closely from the start, moved up with a rush in the last eighth and, taking the lead, held on gamely when challenged and just lasted long enough to withstand MAN O'WAR'S challenge. The latter began slowly, moved up steadily to the stretch turn, where he got into close quarters, then came to the outside in the final eighth and, responding gamely to punishment, was gaining in the closing strides. GOLDEN BROOM showed great speed in pacemaking, but tired when challenged. CAPT. ALCOCK began slowly and closed a big gap. ARMISTICE ran well from a poor beginning. DONNACONA ran forwardly in the early running, was carried wide on the stretch turn and tired.

Scratched—Peace Pennant, 112; Ten Can, 112.

The race was the first and only official encounter between Mrs. Sarah Jeffords' Golden Broom and Riddle's Man o' War. Golden Broom was fresh off a victory in the Saratoga Special where he beat Wildair, a promising young colt from the H.P. Whitney barn.

The race was marred by a horrendous start, a half mile of severe traffic troubles and a stretch drive which featured the tiring Golden Broom serving as an unwitting accomplice in a well-laid trap set by Bill Knapp on the winner, Upset. The fast closing Man o' War and his rider, James Loftus, simply ran out of ground, passing the Whitney charge a few strides beyond the finish line.

The unfortunate result dampened the victory party at the Riddles' Saratoga summer home that sat one block from the track on Union Street. There, Elizabeth Riddle had prepared a special cake with Man o' War's name in fancy frosting. This marked the only time such confection would go unappreciated.

> *For Man o' War was, if not more than a horse, then more than a horse had ever been before.*
>
> *Years later Willie Knapp, who pocketed him with Upset and beat him for his only defeat, was to say, "If I'd known what he was to become, I'd have let him out." It would only have changed the phrasing, not the magnitude of Man o' War's story.*
>
> *Joe H. Palmer,*
> *American Race Horses 1947*

Man o' War finished his first racing season with an overpowering victory in the six furlong Futurity Stakes at Belmont Park, leaving him the undisputed champion of his division. His performances prompted comparisons with the best juveniles known to the American turf which included the great colts Commando and Colin from J.R. Keene's famed Castleton Stud.

Man o' War also drew increasingly large crowds to see him race. Before the running of the Futurity, so many fans pressed into the paddock to get a closer look at the exciting new star that his handlers could hardly push through the mob.

As good as he was at two, Man o' War had not yet set a track record nor had he been tested beyond a sprint distance. All of that changed in a big way the following spring when the massive chestnut, now more than 16 hands, began the most spectacular season of racing in American history.

Over the course of 148 days, Man o' War captured 11 major stakes by a total of 165 lengths. His brush with the rugged Whitney colt John P. Grier in the 1 1/8 mile Dwyer Stakes at Aqueduct was the only time he was ever extended. The two fought neck and neck for the first mile, and at the eighth pole, only 220 yards from home, Grier led the champion by a slight margin. But passing this pole, Man o' War showed his great heart and pulled away to win.

The white eighth post with gold orb atop that marked the start of the decisive ground in this historic race is still preserved near the clubhouse at the "new" Aqueduct facility. It is known, simply, as the "Man o' War Pole."

Throughout the summer of 1920, sportswriters linked Red's name with that of Babe Ruth, who was enjoying the first of his many glorious seasons with the New York Yankees. Almost in rhythm, the two athletes delighted their fans with one gargantuan performance after the other.

Like his baseball counterpart, Red had a colossal appetite. It was said that he consumed 12 quarts of oats on ordinary days and 12 1/2 on the days he raced – three quarts a day more than that of the average racehorse in training. Gentle as a cow in his stall, Big Red was transformed into a dynamo as soon as he was let out. Riddle called him "a party horse."

Opponents were soon in short supply and it was the clock that became Man o' War's best measure. Big Red did not just break time records that year; he shattered them, despite being under firm and constant restraint by his riders. By season's end, he held the American or world records for eight, nine, 11, 12, and 13 furlongs. On a number of occasions the interior fractions from the front-running Man o' War were clocked in times that would have broken American or world sprint records as well.

Table 1

"THE PERFECT STORM"
MAN O' WAR'S THREE-YEAR-OLD RACING SEASON OF 1920

Date	Track/ Cond.		Race/ Purse		Distance	Time	Weight	Record time distinctions & placers (weight carried)
5/18	Pim	fst	Preakness	29K	1 1/8 mi.	1:51.3	126	1 1/2 lengths over Upset (122 lbs.), Wildair (114)
5/28	Bel	fst	Withers	5.8K	1 mile	1:35.4	118	New American Record / 2 lengths over Wildair (118)
6/12	Bel	fst	Belmont	9.2K	1 3/8 mi.	2:14.1	126	New World Record / 20 lengths over Donnaconna (126)
6/22	Jam	gd	Stuyvesant	4.5K	1 mile	1:41.3	135	8 lengths over Yellow Hand (103)
7/10	Aqu	fst	Dwyer	5.5K	1 1/8 mi.	1:49.1	126	New World Record / 1 1/2 lengths over John P. Grier (108)
8/7	Sar	fst	Miller	5.7K	1 3/16 mi.	1:56.3	131	6 lengths over Donnaconna (119), King Albert (114)
8/21	Sar	fst	Travers	12K	1 1/4 mi.	2:01.4	129	Equaled Track Record / 2 1/2 lengths over Upset (123)
9/4	Bel	fst	Lawrence Realization	16K	1 5/8 mi.	2:40.4	126	New World Record / 100 lengths over Hoodwink (116)
9/11	Bel	fst	Jockey Club Gold Cup	6.8K	1 1/2 mi.	2:28.4	118	New American Record / 15 lengths over Damask (108)
9/18	HdG	fst	Potomac H	10K	1 1/16 mi.	1:44.4	138	New Track Record / 1 1/2 lengths over Wildair (108)
10/12	Knw	fst	Kenilworth Park Gold Cup	75K	1 1/4 mi.	2:03	120	New Track Record / 7 lengths over Sir Barton (126)

29

Man o' War works out.

One of the measures of Man o' War's greatness was the depth of talent within his generation. In July 1920, O'Neill Sevier wrote in *The Thoroughbred Record*, "not for a quarter of a century has a single season boasted of so great of a number of high class three-year-olds . . . if Man o' War were out of the way it would look as though we had upward of a dozen top-notch distance-running three-year-olds, every one of them worthy to be called great."

As his colt's reputation continued to soar, Sam Riddle, eager for ever-greater triumphs, began holding what the newspapers described as "board of strategy" meetings with his friends and other track kibitzers. The "board" discussed the races in which Man o' War should be started and how the jockey should be instructed to ride. Feustel, temperamental and proud of his part in the horse's career, considered the sessions as meddling in his affairs. A series of squabbles between trainer and owner followed, but were overshadowed by Red's subsequent victories.

Later in the season, Feustel was further incensed when he discovered that despite the watch he and his help kept over Man o' War, Riddle had hired a private detective to keep an eye on them. As it was, Red's groom, Frank Loftus, was warned to never let the colt out of sight during his working hours. In the evenings, Feustel, his foreman George Conway, and their friends set up a table in front of Man o' War's stall for a nightly game of pitch. When the game was over, Conway slept next to the stall.

In spite of all of this, Riddle was justified in beefing up security for his irreplaceable treasure. For months there were rumors of threats against the horse. After Man o' War's final race against Sir Barton, it was found that his stirrup leathers were intentionally cut but, fortunately, had held for the duration of the contest.

Sam Riddle decided to retire Man o' War from racing at the end of this amazing season. Man o' War had already garnered lifetime earnings of $249,465, an American record. To race him as a four-year-old, race secretaries would continue to add more and more weight, putting him at risk for breaking down.

These two incredible years made Man o' War a national hero and focused world-wide attention on both horse and owner. Riddle was in the process of completing the highest ride any horseman had ever been on, and yet his good standing was not unanimous.

Kentuckians headed by Churchill Downs manager Matt J. Winn were miffed when Glen Riddle Farm announced the juvenile sensation would pass on the mile and one-quarter Derby in early May, considering it too far, too soon in the three-year-old season. More offense was taken when Riddle, after Red easily handled Sir Barton in Canada, turned down a rich match race at Churchill Downs with older handicap star Exterminator.

Afterwards, trackman Winn, who witnessed every running of the Kentucky Derby since Aristides' 1875 victory, whenever asked who was the greatest racehorse, would automatically respond, "Exterminator."

Sour grapes? What else could have driven someone with knowledge of racing to say that?

Sir Barton knocked off Exterminator that summer at Saratoga while giving him weight. Even more important, Exterminator's internal fractions in all of his previous encounters were not in the same ballpark as those of Big Red. "Old Bones," as he was called, did not have the speed to stay in a match race with Man o' War. Riddle's refusal had nothing to do with dodging a worthy challenger but rather doing what he thought was best for his horse. According to Feustel, Red had struck himself in the Potomac at Havre de Grace and had some filling in the leg while preparing for his final race against Sir Barton.

The contemporary journalist showing the greatest antagonism towards Samuel Riddle was Neil Newman, who wrote for *The Thoroughbred Record* and later *The British Bloodhorse Breeders' Review*, sometimes under the pen name of 'Roamer.'

"Despite a lukewarm feeling for Man o' War personally, and irrespective of the antipathy with which I have always regarded his connections, I am nevertheless forced to admit he was a super horse in all that the term implies."

Newman never explained his caustic remarks and on what they were based, but it did underscore the adversarial relationship Sam Riddle endured with some members of the press. Riddle, no shrinking violet, had his own way with words. He quipped that some sportswriters knew only two things about horses: "One end bites and the other end kicks."

To others, however, Riddle was held in much higher regard, an esteemed sportsman of the old school.

J.K.M. Ross, whose father Commander J.K.L. Ross, WWI Royal Canadian Naval hero, owned Sir Barton, wrote in his 1956 book, *Boots and Saddle*:

"Mr. Riddle was very handsome. Every inch a gentleman, he resembled the classic retired British Army general in appearance and had a well-trimmed, military-type mustache to accentuate this illusion. Tall and very straight in his carriage, with a ruddy complexion, which stamped him as a man who spent a great deal of time out of doors, he always gave the impression of extreme physical fitness. Throughout his life, he rode to hounds and . . . once described as 'Sam Riddle, who grins like a possum in that pleasing way of his,' he did, indeed, wear a smile well and often . . .

Samuel D. Riddle was a sharply dressed, mustachioed fellow, usually described in aristocratic terms as having the manner of an English general resembling a Roman senator.

"Mr. Riddle and his gracious, soft-spoken wife owned a home near the (Saratoga) racecourse at the far end of Union Avenue, and they entertained frequently, chiefly with a series of late afternoon parties. Almost invariably, they served mint juleps – perfect juleps in silver mugs thick with frost. At the mention of Mr. Riddle's name, I can still conjure up in my memory the exquisite taste and aroma of that indescribably delightful concoction which was the Riddle specialty."

As Riddle was bringing his brilliant colt's racing career to a close, he was besieged with offers of every description. Cattle and oil baron William T. Waggoner was willing to buy Riddle's treasure at any price. He started with numbers, but was soon offering up a blank check to possess the animal.

"You go to France and bring back the Tomb of Napoleon. You go to India and buy the Taj Mahal. Then I'll put a price on Man o' War." That was the response from Red's unwavering master.

A movie proposal almost reached the stage of signing papers, but it too was rejected after Riddle read the script. "They were going to write a villain into the story!" Riddle declared in a 1937 interview, "and there aren't any villains in Man o' War's story."

Feustel, a man with ambition and a healthy ego, was cast to play himself in the flick. News of its cancellation may have been the final straw in his stormy relationship with Riddle, as he left the services of the latter soon thereafter.

Riddle seemed to be making a statement. Man o' War was not for sale. He wasn't even for rent.

The only exhibition Riddle consented to was a "little" gathering of his friends and neighbors at the Rose Tree Hunt in Media, just outside of Philadelphia. About 30,000 fans also decided to show up that late autumn day, blocking the narrow Delaware County roads with their automobiles. On hand for the event was tennis champion Bill Tilden along with Riddle pal and boxing hero Jack Dempsey. Souvenir hunters started clipping so much hair off Big Red's mane and tail that the Philadelphia police had to rush a sergeant and 10 officers to help guard him.

After the spirited Rose Tree engagement, Man o' War was shipped to Glen Riddle for wintering. He travelled, as he always did, with only his old friend Major Treat as equine company in the horsecar.

In late January 1921, Red was railed to Lexington, where he spent the night in Colonel E.R. Bradley's barn at the old Association track. The next day, with his regular exercise rider, Clyde Gordon, up in the stirrups, he cantered an exhibition mile past a cheering crowd, with Major Treat pacing him. He was then retired, definitely and permanently.

Later that afternoon, Man o' War was vanned from the track to Hinata Stock Farm, just outside of the city, where his second glorious career would soon begin.

One thing is clear: Sam Riddle wanted Big Red to retire as a true champion, and that is precisely what happened.

In his prime – Man o' War is shown in his racing heyday
with Johnny Loftus up.

CHAPTER THREE

PEDIGREE OF A SUPERSTAR

"Hastings was a mean, exasperating, and brilliant neurotic, so fiery with desire for action and competition that he was almost unmanageable . . . When that impetuous competitive fire was later diluted a bit in the heart of Man o' War it resulted in the nearly perfect horse."

Page Cooper and Roger L. Treat, Man o' War 1951

Man o' War's immediate ancestry exemplified more than 20 years of judicious selection and blending of fine bloodstock by the preeminent American breeder, August Belmont II, at his Nursery Stud. Located four miles north of Lexington along the Georgetown Pike, the farm was started by his father in 1885.

Between 1895 and 1908, Belmont acquired all four of Man o' War's second-generation ancestors. He then proceeded to cross their blood, gaining outstanding results in the process – reaching the apex when Man o' War was foaled.

Several months after becoming chairman of the newly founded Jockey Club, Belmont purchased Big Red's paternal grandsire Hastings in 1895 at public auction for a whopping $37,000. Hastings, a colt with a soon-to-be legendary mean streak, was a son of Spendthrift whose own sire, *Australian, was imported to the U.S. as a weanling in 1858. Australian would later stand at R.A. Alexander's Woodburn Farm alongside the immortal Lexington, 19th century America's greatest runner and stallion.

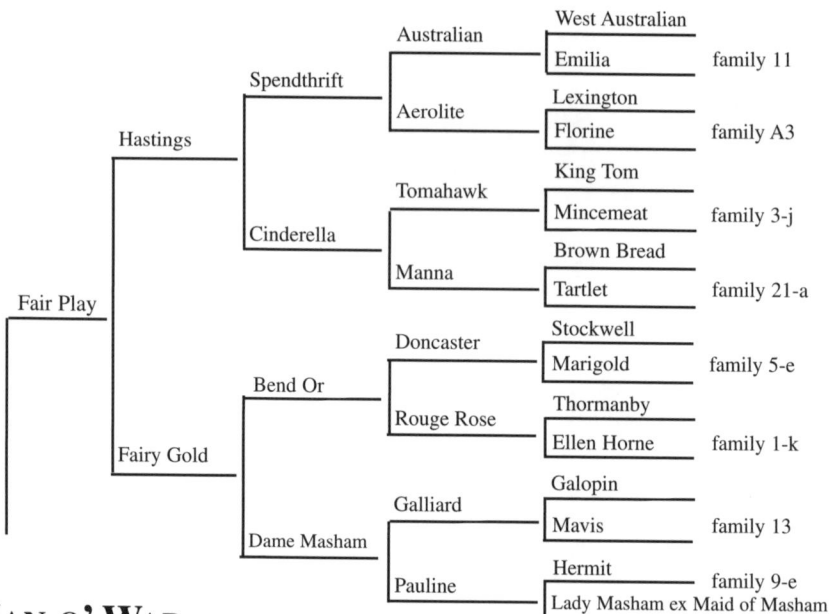
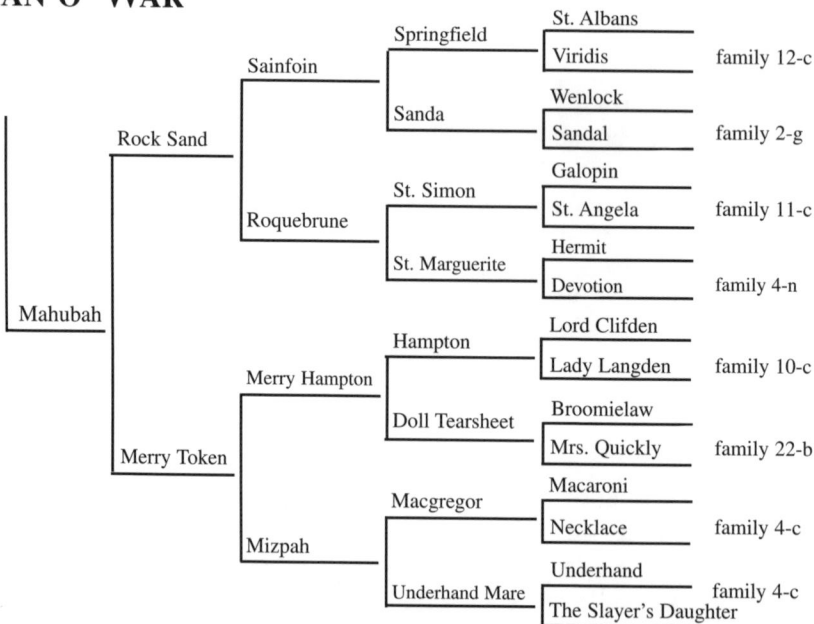

MAN O' WAR

Fair Play
- Hastings
  - Spendthrift
    - Australian
      - West Australian
      - Emilia — family 11
    - Aerolite
      - Lexington
      - Florine — family A3
  - Cinderella
    - Tomahawk
      - King Tom
      - Mincemeat — family 3-j
    - Manna
      - Brown Bread
      - Tartlet — family 21-a
- Fairy Gold
  - Bend Or
    - Doncaster
      - Stockwell
      - Marigold — family 5-e
    - Rouge Rose
      - Thormanby
      - Ellen Horne — family 1-k
  - Dame Masham
    - Galliard
      - Galopin
      - Mavis — family 13
    - Pauline
      - Hermit
      - Lady Masham ex Maid of Masham — family 9-e

Mahubah
- Rock Sand
  - Sainfoin
    - Springfield
      - St. Albans
      - Viridis — family 12-c
    - Sanda
      - Wenlock
      - Sandal — family 2-g
  - Roquebrune
    - St. Simon
      - Galopin
      - St. Angela — family 11-c
    - St. Marguerite
      - Hermit
      - Devotion — family 4-n
- Merry Token
  - Merry Hampton
    - Hampton
      - Lord Clifden
      - Lady Langden — family 10-c
    - Doll Tearsheet
      - Broomielaw
      - Mrs. Quickly — family 22-b
  - Mizpah
    - Macgregor
      - Macaroni
      - Necklace — family 4-c
    - Underhand Mare
      - Underhand
      - The Slayer's Daughter — family 4-c

Belmont paid the lavish price for the juvenile Hastings with an eye toward that year's prestigious Futurity Stakes. Instead, the defiant colt didn't reveal his true ability until a year later when he captured the 30th running of the Belmont Stakes, the marquis event named after his owner's father. Before Hastings, his sire, Spendthrift, and two other sons of Australian were also winners of the Belmont Stakes. Over the next three decades, Belmont succeeded in breeding five more winners of this race, four of these at his Nursery Stud.

Despite competing for mares with Belmont's other highly regarded stallions, Hastings quickly distinguished himself as a sire of quality runners. He led the sires' list in 1901 with only two crops on the track, and repeated that honor in 1908 when his best son, Fair Play, was a three-year-old.

Man o' War's broodmare sire, *Rock Sand, was imported by Belmont during the second half of 1908. An English Triple Crown winner, Rock Sand was a magnificently conformed individual, kind and intelligent, and seemingly devoid of any of the usual nervous tension associated with the breed.

Rock Sand stood four seasons at Nursery Stud (1909-1912). When politics brought a temporary cessation to New York racing, Belmont sold Rock Sand to a French syndicate for $125,000, the same amount he had earlier paid for him. In the interim, Belmont stocked his paddocks with Rock Sand's precious sons and daughters. His male progeny included the champions Rock View and Friar Rock as well as English classic winner Tracery, who Belmont later sold to Argentina for a world record $265,000. Rock Sand's daughters would become even more valuable as the dams of many other important winners, a list that includes Man o' War.

*Fairy Gold and *Merry Token, the respective dams of Man o' War's sire and dam, were both acquired for Belmont by the well-known British turf writer and bloodstock agent William Allison. One of the most influential names in the history of horse brokerage, Allison would play a pivotal role in the shaping of Man o' War's stallion legacy two generations later.

Allison spent about 3,600 guineas (about $18,000) to get the seven-year-old Bend Or mare Fairy Gold for Belmont in 1903. Fairy Gold, a stakes winner in England at two, would become the priceless dam of Man o' War's sire, Fair Play, as well as Belmont Stakes hero Friar Rock.

Allison picked up Merry Token in 1902 for about $200, a far cry in price from Red's other three grandparents. Merry Token was a daughter of Merry Hampton, best known for winning the 1887 English Derby in his first start, but not much else. Merry Token's broodmare sire MacGregor won the 1870 Two Thousand Guineas but was never fashionable at stud either.

Merry Token seems to represent the weakest quarter of Man o' War's pedigree. Moreover, her tail-female line, family number 4-c, was not one known for issuing many quality runners, let alone sires.

It's worth noting that MacGregor, sire of Man o' War's third dam, Mizpah, also descends from the 4-c family. Both Mizpah's sire and dam trace back to a common taproot matriarch Maniac (1806, by Shuttle). I originally dubbed this distinct pedigree pattern where both parents descend in tail-female line to the same influential matron as the 'Formula One Pattern' (Formula One: A Unique Method of Inbreeding, *Owner-Breeder*, March 1995). It can be identified in the pedigrees of a disproportionate number of exceptional runners and producers throughout the history of the breed.

From the eight foals Merry Token produced for Belmont, the one that made her famous was her dark bay Rock Sand filly, aptly named Mahubah which is Arabic for "good greetings, good fortune."

During her short career at the track, Mahubah was trained by Louis Feustel who found her to have exceptional speed but too nervous for her own good. Belmont was convinced that excessive racing was detrimental to a broodmare's subsequent stud career. Much of this stemmed from his well-raced champion filly Beldame and her dismal record as a producer. As a result, Mahubah was returned to Nursery Stud at age three, after one win in five starts. There she began a series of auspicious matings with Fair Play, the only stallion to which she was ever bred.

Fair Play

```
                                    Australian
                   Spendthrift
                                    Aerolite
        Hastings
                                    Tomahawk by KING TOM out of
                                                POCAHONTAS
                   Cinderella
                                    Manna
FAIR PLAY
                                    Doncaster by STOCKWELL out of
                                                POCAHONTAS
                   Bend Or
                                    Rouge Rose
        Fairy Gold
                                    Galliard
                   Dame Masham
                                    Pauline
```

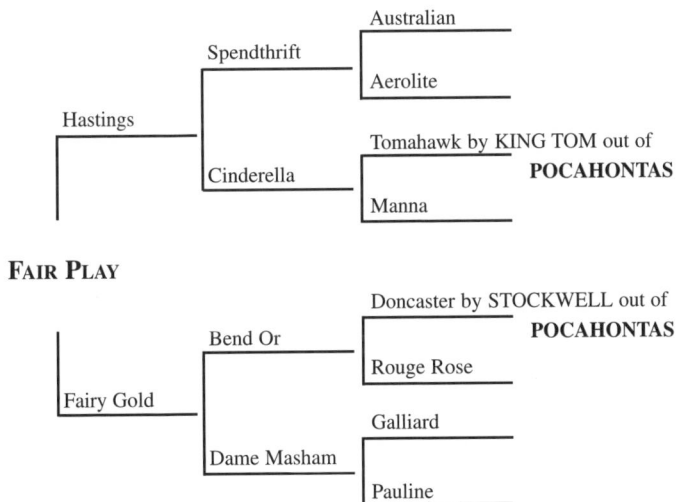

Had Fair Play not been from the same crop as the undefeated Colin, a juggernaut from the powerful J.R. Keene stable, it is possible he would have been heralded as one of the greatest runners of all time. Fair Play suffered a total of five defeats to Colin, the last of these by a head in the 1908 Belmont Stakes run in a driving rainstorm. Once Colin was retired midway through his sophomore season, Fair Play's career took off, recording victories in the Brooklyn Derby, the Lawrence Realization, and the Jerome Handicap, as well as several other added money events.

Fair Play had a flaming golden coat and a regal spirit, but he could be petulant. When sent to England for an ambitious four-year-old campaign, his strong personality turned bitter resulting in a very unrewarding sojourn. Nevertheless, upon his return to Kentucky to begin his career as a stallion, Belmont was quoted in a February 1910 issue of the *Racing Form* as saying:

"Fair Play is the best horse I have ever owned – I expect him to show by his get that he is the superior of his sire (Hastings), Rock Sand, and all the other sires I have had."

These were confident words and ones that Fair Play would justify with time.

If one evaluates the pedigrees of the stallions at Nursery Stud and those of their best sons and daughters, what becomes apparent is the marked accumulation of strains from the illustrious family of Pocahontas, arguably the most influential English broodmare of the 19th century. This was the prevailing breeding strategy Belmont practiced throughout his long, celebrated career.

Rayon d'Or, Belmont's first successful sire, had Pocahontas as his granddam and generally sired his best offspring when his master bred him to mares carrying additional strains of this great matriarch, particularly through her sons Stockwell, King Tom and Rataplan.

Hastings' dam, Cinderella, is a granddaughter of King Tom. When Hastings went to stud, virtually all of his best progeny were out of dams carrying complementary strains of Pocahontas. This, of course, included his best son Fair Play.

Rock Sand's pedigree was a cornucopia of Pocahontas strains, a total of five through her three best sons.

Rock Sand

```
                                        ┌ St. Albans by STOCKWELL out of
                          Springfield ──┤              POCAHONTAS
                                        └ Viridis
             Sainfoin ────┤
                                        ┌ Wenlock by RATAPLAN out of
                          Sanda ────────┤              POCAHONTAS
                                        └ Sandal by STOCKWELL out of
                                                       POCAHONTAS
ROCK SAND ───┤
                                        ┌ Galopin
                          St. Simon ────┤
                                        └ St. Angela by KING TOM out of
                                                       POCAHONTAS
             Roquebrune ──┤
                                        ┌ Hermit
                          St. Marguerite┤
                                        └ Devotion by STOCKWELL out of
                                                       POCAHONTAS
```

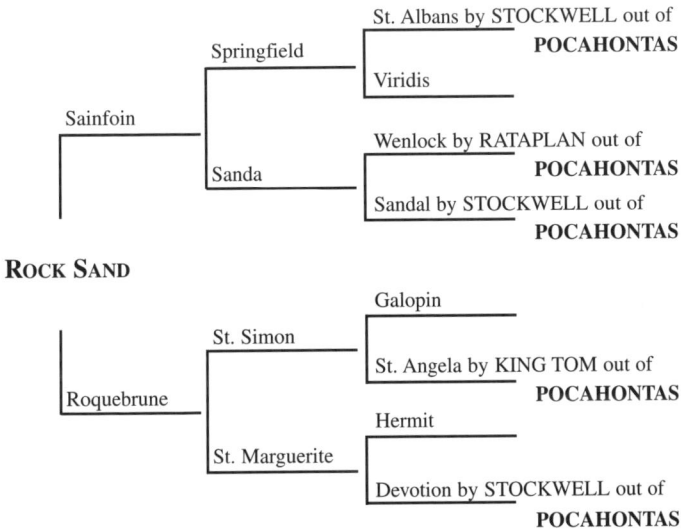

The Fair Play-Rock Sand cross represents August Belmont's ultimate recipe. This cross proved to be one of the most powerful affinities in the history of the American Thoroughbred. Several years after Belmont's death, his son, Capt. Raymond Belmont, confirmed his father's overall plan to *The Thoroughbred Record*, remarking, "Fair Play's success has been due mainly to the intensification of the blood of Stockwell and his dam, Pocahontas, through Rock Sand."

In all, Man o' War carried a total of nine strains of Pocahontas: two from Fair Play, five from Rock Sand and two more from Merry Hampton.

Fair Play became one of the most dominant stallions of his era, leading the sires list three times (1920, 1924 and 1927). It was his remarkable affinity with Rock Sand that represented the overwhelming majority of his influence.

	Total	Stakes Winners (% SWs)
All Fair Play offspring	260	47 (18%)
Fair Play offspring with Rock Sand blood	81 (31%)	24 (30%)
Fair Play offspring without Rock Sand blood	179 (69%)	23 (13%)

Fair Play sired a total of 260 offspring, 47 (18 percent) were stakes winners. Eighty-one of his offspring carried the blood of Rock Sand (appearing as broodmare sire, sire of the broodmare sire or sire of the second dam). In other words, 81 of 260 (31 percent) of Fair Play's total foals carried the Fair Play-Rock Sand cross. Remarkably, 24 (30 percent) of these 81 individuals went on to become stakes winners.

If one then takes into account Belmont's aversion to the racing of fillies, the Fair Play-Rock Sand 'nick' becomes even stronger.

	Total	Stakes Winners (% SWs)
Fair Play offspring with Rock Sand blood	81	24 (30%)
Males	30	19 (63%)
Females	51	5 (10%)

Of the 81 offspring with the Fair Play-Rock Sand cross, 30 were colts and geldings. Nineteen of these became stakes winners (an incredible 63 percent). The other 51 were fillies, only five of which became stakes winners (10 percent). What might have appeared to be a powerful sex bias was really Belmont's tendency to under-race his fillies. Indeed, the large majority of Fair Play fillies out of Rock Sand mares show no record of ever having been raced.

Fair Play was the first stallion to sire six winners of $100,000 or more. Five of these had first or second dams by Rock Sand.

Table 2		Top Representatives of the Fair Play - Rock Sand Cross
MAD HATTER	c. 1916	Male Handicap Champion, $194,525, Jockey Club Gold Cup / Sire (22 SWs)
MAN o' WAR	c. 1917	Horse of the Century, $249,465 / Leading sire 1926 (64 SWs)
SPORTING BLOOD	c. 1918	Travers S., Latonia Championship S., etc., $49,864/ Sire (4 SWs)
CHATTERTON	c. 1919	Falls City H., etc., $26,565 / Leading sire 1932 (11 SWs)
MY PLAY	c. 1919	Jockey Club Gold Cup, Aqueduct H., etc., $32,490 / Sire (8 SWs)
DUNLIN	c. 1920	Hopeful S., Dwyer S., Knickerbocker S., etc., $92,919/ Sire (8 SWs)
MAD PLAY	c. 1921	Belmont S., Brooklyn H., Saratoga Cup, etc, $136,432
FAIRMOUNT	g. 1921	American Steeplechase Hall of Fame, $75,075
CHANCE PLAY	c. 1923	Horse of the Year at 4, $137,946 / Leading sire twice 1935 & 1944 (23 SWs)
CHANCE SHOT	c. 1924	Belmont S., Saratoga Special, Withers S., $142,946 / Sire (22 SWs)

As early as March of 1920 (before Man o' War's three-year-old season began), *The Thoroughbred Record* reported that buyers of Thoroughbred stock were specifically looking for prospects with this cross.

The Fair Play-Rock Sand 'nick' actually represented the reverse of an already successful affinity for Belmont. Rock Sand mated to Golden View (Fair Play's full sister) produced the Feustel-trained three-year-old champion of 1913, Rock View. Several years after that, Belmont bred Rock Sand to Fairy Gold and got the 1916 three-year-old champion, Friar Rock.

```
                Sainfoin                              Hastings
  ROCK SAND                            Fair Play
                Roquebrune                            FAIRY GOLD

  FRIAR ROCK                           MAN O' WAR
     1913                                  1917

                Bend Or                               ROCK SAND
  FAIRY GOLD                           Mahubah
                Dame Masham                           Merry Token
```

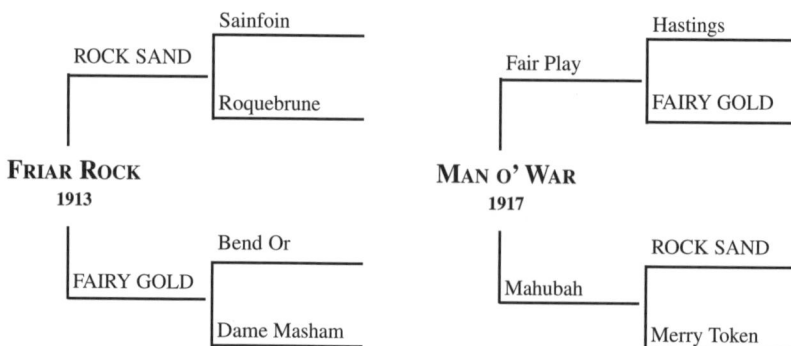

The union of Fair Play with Mahubah produced a total of five off-spring. The oldest, a filly foaled in 1915 named Masda, was turned over to Hall of Fame trainer Sam Hildreth, who had previously conditioned Friar Rock for Belmont. Like her dam, Masda was found to be blazing fast, but so difficult to handle that at Hildreth's suggestion the chestnut filly was sold early in her three-year-old campaign. She eventually joined the broodmare band of Harry Payne Whitney, ultimately gaining her greatest fame as the third dam of 1946 Triple Crown winner Assault.

Mahubah

Mahubah failed to conceive after the birth of Masda, but after a barren season returned to foal Man o' War in 1917. A year later, she foaled Playfellow, a bay colt Belmont sold as a weanling for $1,800 as his attention continued to focus on the war effort. Playfellow only enjoyed a modest career at the track ($4,764 and two wins from eight starts) and had no impact at stud.

In 1919, Mahubah foaled another bay colt, this one named My Play. Like Playfellow, My Play was also sold early in life. Slow to mature, he finally became a multiple stakes winner at age four and then concluded his racing career a year later with a victory in the Jockey Club Gold Cup. Sire of several important offspring, My Play and his much more famous older sibling became the first pair of full brothers to both sire the winners of over $100,000.

Mirabelle, Mahubah's second chestnut daughter and her last foal, arrived in 1920. Man o' War's exploits with the Riddle camp made his younger sister a very valuable filly. Nevertheless, Mirabelle was a small and rather frail individual who was returned to Nursery Stud after only two unplaced juvenile starts. Eventually, she was purchased at Belmont's dispersal sale by Joseph E. Widener's Elmendorf Farm in 1925 for $33,000. At stud, she was a useful broodmare without producing anything truly exceptional.

Mahubah lived for another 11 years after producing Mirabelle, but, despite all efforts of expert veterinarians called in, she remained permanently barren.

Such was the genetic heritage of the great Man o' War. There is satisfaction in knowing his was not the randomness of a "freak," but of a pedigree that reflects the well-measured practices of a master breeder, from a potent American sire line, of otherwise classic English origins.

CHAPTER FOUR

A Strategy Takes Shape

"The homing instinct is as strong in man as in pigeons. Mr. Riddle's Glen Riddle Farm in Pennsylvania is one of the most attractive places anywhere, and the temptation to establish Man o' War there was great.

"But Mr. Riddle has said when he refused big sums for Man o' War that he held the Fair Play stallion in trust for the American people as an invaluable instrument for the improvement of the breed.

"He put aside his personal preference when he decided to establish him in Kentucky, because he feels that in Kentucky Man o' War will have the best chance to demonstrate quickly whether he is to succeed or fail as a stock horse."

O'Neil Sevier
The Thoroughbred Record, November, 1920

Plans for Man o' War's stud career began to take shape during the latter half of his spectacular three-year-old season. Samuel Riddle and Walter Jeffords formed a new breeding alliance with the goal of getting Red off to the best start at stud as possible.

The alliance adopted a four-part strategy. First, Riddle and Jeffords assembled a team of the best employees and advisors available.

Second, they assembled an impressive broodmare band with pedigrees affording Man o' War the best opportunity to produce champions. Thirdly, they limited Big Red's outside bookings. Lastly, they built a showplace stud farm that would become their base of operations.

Elizabeth Daingerfield was appointed Big Red's stallion manager. She engaged the services of well-known British bloodstock agent William Allison to acquire broodmares for Riddle and Jeffords best suited as initial mates for their exciting new franchise. According to *The Thoroughbred Record*, Allison was instructed to "buy a number of mares on the British market, whose blood will nick with that of the great son of Fair Play."

At the 1920 Tattersalls Newmarket December Sale, Allison purchased a handful of young females with prices ranging from a few thousand dollars to close to $12,000. Certainly not cheap by the standards of the day, these broodmare prospects would go on to share in a significant portion of Man o' War's success.

Man o' War spent his first two seasons at stud in Kentucky at Hinata Stock Farm, located about six miles north of Lexington at the junction of Russell Cave Road and Iron Works Pike, where Daingerfield, an exceptional horsewoman, was manager. Her own farm, Haylands, sat adjacent to Hinata and was home to High Time, a future influential sire in his own right. High Time's success may be attributed to Daingerfield's success in getting him the right mares, despite his intimidating pedigree – three strains of Domino within just three generations.

Man o' War had now reached his full height of 16.2 1/4 hands. He was placed under the care of John "Buck" Buckner who had groomed the great Castleton stallions of James R. Keene where Daingerfield's father was manager. Buck was known for his slow movements and gentle voice and Red took to him immediately.

In late May 1922, the mighty chestnut was transferred to his owners' newly built Faraway Farm just two miles north of Hinata. Russell Cave Road, a small dusty road at the time, connected the two farms.

This was now Red's permanent home and his showplace until his death in 1947. The 780 acres of land that became Riddle's and the

Jeffords' Faraway Farm was recommended by Daingerfield. She then supervised the construction of the barns, paddocks and other structures. The tract was taken from the back of Louis Lee Haggin's Mt. Brilliant Farm, both estates lying along Huffman Mill Pike. As things were situated, the granite monument at Mt. Brilliant that marked the grave of Domino, possibly the fastest horse of the 19th century, stood almost within sight of Big Red's spacious new quarters.

Man o' War was not advertised for public service in 1921 but in the fall of that year Riddle announced that in 1922 he would offer 10 seasons to outside mares, at $2,500. He stood at this figure in 1922, 1923, and 1924, with no return privilege and with the stipulation that no mare could be bred more than three times in one season. Red's fee was the same as Friar Rock's in California and Broomstick's at the stud of H.P. Whitney, tops in America.

Elizabeth Daingerfield was the daughter of Foxhall A. Daingerfield, the manager (1893-1913) of the illustrious Castleton Stud owned by his brother-in-law James R. Keene. It was Daingerfield with his clever eye for pedigrees who was responsible for the matings that produced many of the best racehorses of that era. Most of these key matings resulted from a series of acquisitions made by the very same William Allison, whom Keene had commissioned to assemble a choice band of English-bred broodmares.

Allison selected an assortment of broodmare prospects at the Tattersalls December sales of 1891 and 1892. When imported to America these mares founded the families of many of the most influential sires of that era including Peter Pan and his sons Pennant and Black Toney, as well as Sweep and Broomstick. A decade later, as previously mentioned, Allison purchased the dam of Fair Play and the granddam of Man o' War for August Belmont II.

Given this amazing resume, commissioning the now elder English gentleman to select choice European broodmares on behalf of the Man o' War team was "a no-brainer."

Allison was long considered one of England's leading commentators on racing and breeding. He was best known as the advocate of C. Bruce Lowe's 'Figure System' and he edited and published Lowe's book after the author's death. The controversial theory was scorned by a number of prominent American breeders who considered its principles preposterous, or worse, capable of the ruination of the breed. Nevertheless, the Figure System gained sufficient interest both in America and abroad to warrant its inclusion within the pedigrees of several important Thoroughbred sales catalogs.

The Figure System suggests that the pedigrees of superior race-horses usually demonstrate the accumulation of certain female lines that are more valuable than the rest. These preferred families were identified and numbered by Lowe according to success in the English classics. The result was an approach to breeding that proposed the utilization of select female lines and the exclusion of others. The best 'running lines,' as they were called, originated from families 1, 2, 3, 4, and 5, while the best sire blood was said to arise from families 3, 8, 11, 13, and 14.

Lowe's *Breeding Race Horses By The Figure System* was first published in 1895. A second edition in 1913 included much more of Allison's input than the initial volume. Among the dozens of eschewed female lines in the book were the original American tribes, many of them illustrious but unable to be traced back to the foundation mares of England.

In 1913 England's Jockey Club passed the Jersey Act that prohibited many Thoroughbreds from the U.S. and Australia from being registered in the *English Stud Book*. The Jersey Act was a reaction to a perceived economic threat when waves of anti-gambling laws across the U.S. sent a surplus of horses to Europe, creating a potential menace to the precious English stallion market. When English breeders became sufficiently alarmed, so-called 'impurities' within the American Stud Book were cited as justification for the controversial measure. American 'half-breds' were allowed to race, but not to breed in countries wishing to abide by English rules.

At the epicenter of the conflict was the great stallion Lexington. The female line of his grandsire, Timoleon, could not be traced "without flaw" to horses already accepted in earlier volumes of the General Stud Book and Lexington was thus barred from its entry. Lexington's blood represented the backbone of early 20th century American pedigrees and the Jersey Act effectively deflated the value of most American stock, raising the ire of its breeders.

Part of the fallout from all of this was heightened rancor towards the discriminatory dogma of Lowe and his disciple, Allison. It was guilt by perceived association, even though Allison's international bloodstock agency was dependent on the liberties of free and unhindered trade between nations. A former lawyer, Allison never clarified the differences between his breeding theories and his business policies and became a polarizing figure throughout much of the racing world.

Despite his endorsement of Lowe's Figure System, Allison did not make its principles a major criterion in the selection of broodmares for Man o' War. By examining and comparing the bloodstock Allison acquired for Riddle and Jeffords, it is possible to ascertain the breeding strategies he did have in mind.

Perhaps, the finest pedigree among the mares Allison bought for Riddle belonged to *Lady Comfey, by Roi Herode, an unraced three-quarter sister to 1920 St. Leger Stakes winner Caligula (by Roi Herode's son The Tetrarch) and to 1919 Irish Oaks winner Snow Maiden. This was a fashionable pedigree for this time period. Lady Comfey was from Bruce Lowe's family number 7, a supposedly non-preferred line. Allison paid 880 guineas ($3,382) for her.

From six foals by Man o' War, Lady Comfey produced three stakes winners. By far, the best of these was her first, American Flag, a champion at three in 1925 when he was the first of a trio of Big Red's sons to win the Belmont Stakes. Had it not been for Fair Play's head loss to Colin in 1908, American Flag's victory would have represented an unprecedented fifth consecutive generation of Belmont winners in male line, starting with Spendthrift in 1879.

The most expensive mare Allison purchased was *Batanoea for whom he paid 3,000 guineas ($11,529). She was another unraced daughter of Roi Herode, in foal to Phalaris' half brother Hainault, but one devoid of any close family relations to superior individuals. Allison, it would seem, was specifically looking for well-built daughters of Roi Herode to send to Big Red's court.

Roi Herode

Roi Herode was a French stakes winner with a rare gray coat who stood in Ireland. He descended from the same family as the foundation stallion Bend Or, broodmare sire of Fair Play, Man o' War's sire. The cross of Man o' War with Roi Herode mares, then, created 5x5 inbreeding to their common matron, Rouge Rose, the dam of Bend Or and the third dam of Roi Herode. Breeding Man o' War to Roi Herode line mares represented a reverse of the cross that produced Roi Herode's premiere offspring, the undefeated champion and leading sire The Tetrarch, who was out of a Bend Or line mare.

Batanoea's tail female line also shared family relations with Man o' War since her fifth dam, St. Marguerite, was also the grandam of Rock Sand, Man o' War's broodmare sire. This created 5x6 inbreeding to St. Marguerite, winner of the 1882 One Thousand Guineas and the tap-root matriarch of family number 4-n.

For the Jeffords, Batanoea produced two stakes winners from three foals with Man o' War including their daughter, Gazelle Handicap winner Corvette.

CORVETTE

Man o' War	Fair Play	Hastings	Spendthrift
			Cinderella
		Fairy Gold	Bend Or out of **ROUGE ROSE**
			Dame Masham
	Mahubah	Rock Sand	Sainfoin
			Roquebrune out of **ST. MARGUERITE**
		Merry Token	Merry Hampton
			Mizpah
Batanoea	Roi Herode	Le Samaritain	Le Sancy
			Clementina
		Roxelane	War Dance
			Rose of York out of **ROUGE ROSE**
	Pink Clover	Melton	Master Kildare
			Violet Melrose
		Trefle	Sainfoin
			Cimiez out of Antibes out of **ST. MARGUERITE**

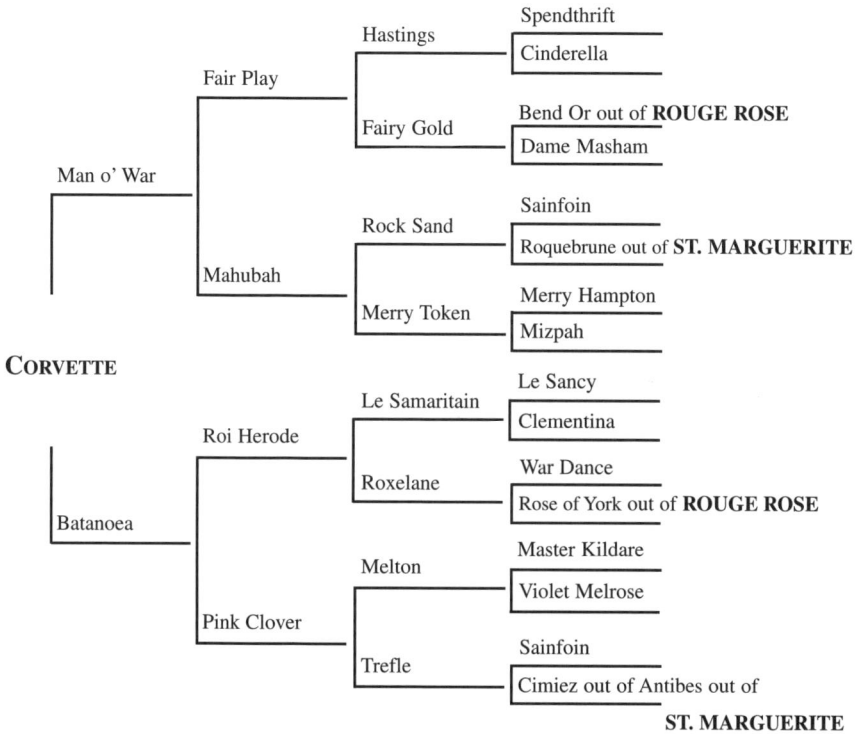

Similarly, the pedigree of *Santissima by St. Angelo, another broodmare acquisition from the 1920 Tattersalls sale ($1,998), featured St. Marguerite as her third dam.

Another Allison purchase for the Jeffords camp was *Bathing Girl, a five-year-old daughter of Spearmint in foal to Harry of Hereford, a non-stakes winning full brother to foundation stallion Swynford. She was another purchase who had never raced. Her older full brother, *Over There, was a disqualified winner of the 1919 Lawrence Realization before running second in the Jerome Handicap. Otherwise, her family, number 11-g, was undistinguished for quite a few generations. Allison spent about $3,075 to secure her.

What seems to have been the key to Bathing Girl's pedigree was that she was out of a daughter of the influential sire Sundridge, whose dam (Sierra) was a full sister to Sainfoin, sire of Man o' War's broodmare sire, Rock Sand.

Bathing Girl foaled the Harry of Hereford filly Annette K. not long after arriving from England in 1921. When bred to Man o' War soon thereafter, Bathing Girl produced Seaplane, future granddam of Hall of Famer, Eight Thirty.

In turn, Annette K., when bred to Man o' War, produced War Glory, a very good three-year-old colt who captured a number of important races including the Lawrence Realization and Dwyer Stakes. Annette K. was also the dam of the unraced Sweep filly Brushup who later produced War Admiral, Man o' War's best son. War Admiral's greatest victory was the 1937 Belmont Stakes when he became America's fourth Triple Crown winner while breaking his sire's 17-year-old Belmont Park track record for the mile and one-half.

In the years to follow, the pedigrees of an impressive list of major international winners featured the brother-sister cross of Sainfoin and Sierra. It was a pattern the Man o' War team would themselves later revisit with further success.

Three years later, Allison assisted Jeffords in importing *Escuina, a French-bred daughter of the relatively obscure sire Ecouen. Escuina's pedigree was highlighted by her very influential third dam, Fairy Gold (family number 9-e). Since Fairy Gold was dam of Man o' War's sire Fair Play, mating Ecuina to Man o' War created a 3x4 inbreeding to Fairy Gold. For good measure, Ecouen also descended from the same family as Fair Play, since his fifth dam Maid of Masham was also the fifth dam of Fair Play. This is illustrated in Fair Play's family tree (Figure 1).

Escuina produced two stakes winners from six foals with Man o' War including his best daughter, Bateau. A champion at both three and four, as a four-year-old (1929) she beat males in the Suburban Handicap, the Whitney Stakes at Saratoga, and the rich Southern Maryland Handicap at Bowie. Her Suburban Handicap win was a three-heads finish with Petee-Wrack and Toro in one of the most thrilling races of the decade. In her career finale at Bowie, she nailed Whitney's Victorian on the wire.

Figure 1 THE DESCENDANTS OF MAID OF MASHAM: THE FAMILY OF FAIR PLAY

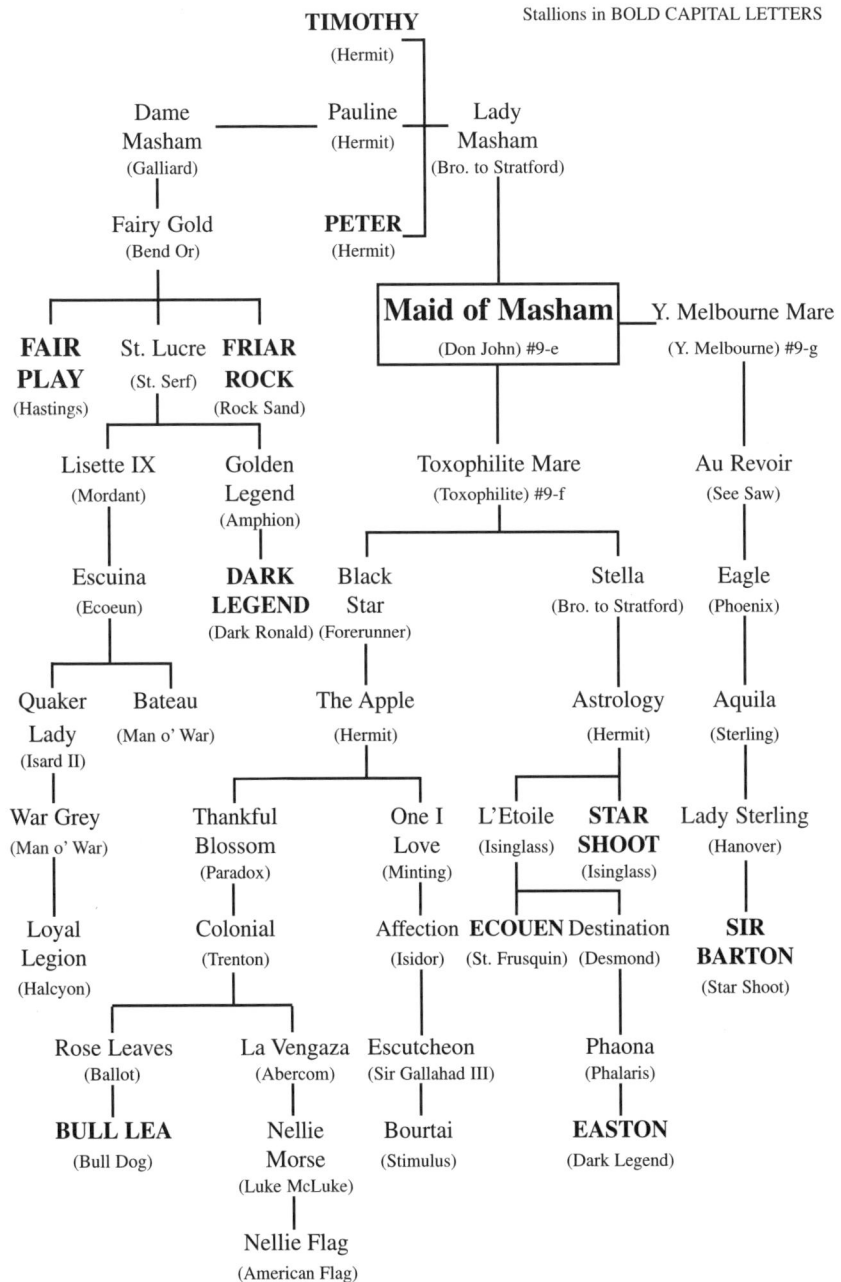

Stallions in BOLD CAPITAL LETTERS

TIMOTHY
(Hermit)

Dame Masham (Galliard) — Pauline (Hermit) — Lady Masham (Bro. to Stratford)

Fairy Gold (Bend Or)

PETER (Hermit)

Maid of Masham (Don John) #9-e — Y. Melbourne Mare (Y. Melbourne) #9-g

FAIR PLAY (Hastings) — St. Lucre (St. Serf) — **FRIAR ROCK** (Rock Sand)

Lisette IX (Mordant) — Golden Legend (Amphion)

Toxophilite Mare (Toxophilite) #9-f

Au Revoir (See Saw)

Escuina (Ecoeun)

DARK LEGEND (Dark Ronald) — Black Star (Forerunner)

Stella (Bro. to Stratford)

Eagle (Phoenix)

Quaker Lady (Isard II) — Bateau (Man o' War)

The Apple (Hermit)

Astrology (Hermit)

Aquila (Sterling)

War Grey (Man o' War)

Thankful Blossom (Paradox)

One I Love (Minting) — L'Etoile (Isinglass) — **STAR SHOOT** (Isinglass)

Lady Sterling (Hanover)

Loyal Legion (Halcyon)

Colonial (Trenton)

Affection (Isidor) — **ECOUEN** (St. Frusquin) — Destination (Desmond)

SIR BARTON (Star Shoot)

Rose Leaves (Ballot) — La Vengaza (Abercom) — Escutcheon (Sir Gallahad III)

Phaona (Phalaris)

BULL LEA (Bull Dog)

Nellie Morse (Luke McLuke) — Bourtai (Stimulus)

EASTON (Dark Legend)

Nellie Flag (American Flag)

57

BATEAU

- **Man o' War**
  - Fair Play
    - Hastings
      - Spendthrift
      - Cinderella
    - **Fairy Gold**
      - Bend Or
      - Dame Masham out of PAULINE out of LADY MASHAM out of **MAID OF MASHAM**
  - Mahubah
    - Rock Sand
      - Sainfoin
      - Roquebrune
    - Merry Token
      - Merry Hampton
      - Mizpah
- Escuina
  - Ecouen
    - St. Frusquin
      - St. Simon
      - Isabel
    - L'Etoile
      - Isinglass
      - Astrology out of Stella out of Toxophilite Mare out of **MAID OF MASHAM**
  - Lisette IX
    - Mordant
      - War Dance
      - Magdala
    - St. Lucre
      - St. Serf
      - **Fairy Gold** out of Dame Masham out of PAULINE out of LADY MASHAM out of **MAID OF MASHAM**

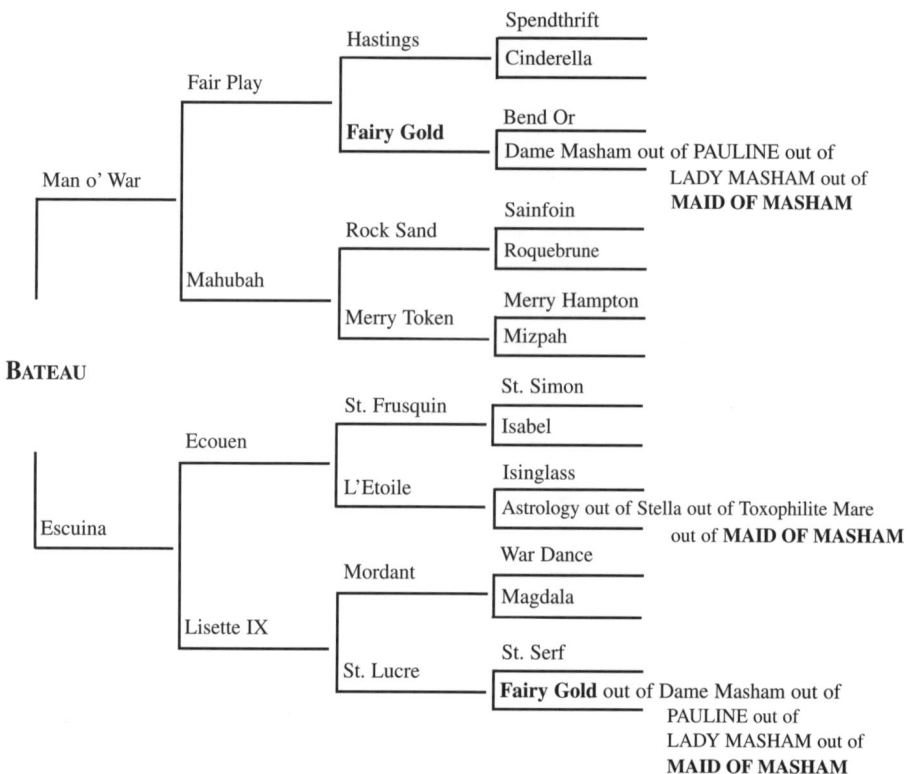

Since several of these mares had family numbers not advocated by Lowe's Figure System, its involvement in Allison's decision making appears unlikely. Instead, the common feature among all of these mares was the presence of complementary strains to the best families in Man o' War's own pedigree. In other words, a breeding strategy keying on the formation of female family inbreeding patterns appears to have been the intent.

Allison died during the summer of 1925 when Red's first crop were three-year-olds. It is unfortunate that he never lived long enough to know of all the exceptional racehorses Man o' War would sire from the mares he purchased for Riddle and Jeffords.

While Allison was buying mares in England, Daingerfield was assembling their American counterparts. She, too, appears to have selected broodmares whose union with Man o' War typically created female family inbreeding patterns. This seems fitting since those same nuances were commonly seen in the auspicious pedigrees designed by her father, Major Daingerfield, at Castleton Stud several decades earlier.

Among the first American-bred mares purchased for Riddle's and Jeffords' account were Star Fancy and Christmas Star, daughters of leading American sire *Star Shoot. Both had exceptional family relations.

The unraced Star Fancy was bred by John E. Madden who had previously furnished Sam Riddle with the multiple stakes winning Yankee Witch. Star Fancy was a half sister to 1918 Clark Handicap winner Beaverkill and her third dam was the bountiful matriarch Sallie McClelland, granddam of 1913 Handicap Triple Crown winner Whisk Broom II. Of additional interest in Star Fancy's pedigree was her obscure broodmare sire Migraine, a half-brother to Man o' War's paternal grandsire Hastings. Crossing Hastings' grandson Man o' War with a granddaughter of Migraine created inbreeding to their common dam, *Cinderella.

Star Fancy, to the cover of Man o' War, produced three foals for Riddle. Two of them, Gun Boat and Crusader, were stakes winners.

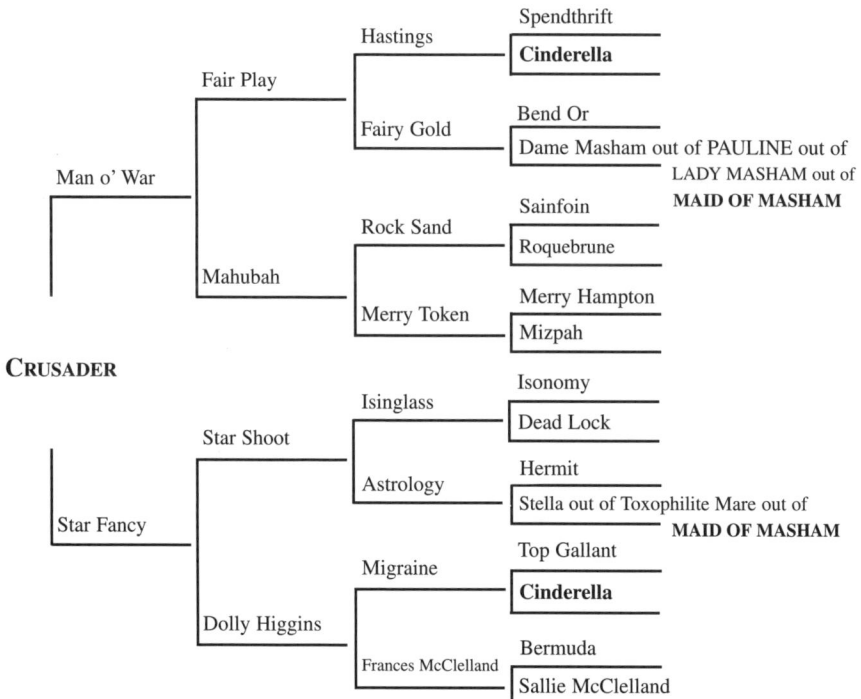

Courtesy Keeneland Library

Crusader

Crusader was named 1926 Horse of the Year at the age of three when he became his sire's second son in as many years to win the Belmont Stakes. He also beat older horses on several occasions that year including the Suburban Handicap and the Jockey Club Gold Cup. The following season, Crusader became the first of only two horses to ever win consecutive runnings of the Suburban. He was an outstanding mudder who would have enjoyed an even better race record (18 wins in 42 starts) if not for some unruliness at the post which, combined with a lack of early speed, seemed to often get him into trouble. Unfortunately, just as Crusader was reaching the apex of his career, he was severely kicked prior to the start of the 1927 Brooklyn Handicap (by the winner, Peanuts) and was never the same great runner after that. He was inducted into Racing's Hall of Fame in 1995.

Stakes-placed Christmas Star was a half-sister to Running Water and a full sister to Addie M., both winners of the Alabama Stakes. Christmas Star was already the dam of Escoba, by Broomstick, one of the best juvenile colts from the 1917 season, when she was acquired for the Jeffords account.

The choice of Star Shoot mares for Man o' War made sense for several reasons. The first and most obvious is that, in 1920, Star Shoot was the leading American stallion of his day with five sire titles over the previous nine years. He was also an outstanding sire of fillies, suggesting he would soon become an important broodmare sire as well. Additionally, breeding the daughters of Star Shoot to Man o' War created inbreeding to the family of Fair Play and Star Shoot through their common matriarch, Maid of Masham (see Figure 1).

Courtesy Keeneland Library

Star Shoot

To the cover of Man o' War, Christmas Star produced the small but talented chestnut colt Mars. At two, he ran the fastest mile to date by a juvenile (1:37) in the Junior Champion at Aqueduct. For three seasons, Jeffords' Mars battled Riddle's Crusader beating him in the Travers but later falling to him in the Jockey Club Gold Cup and the rich Riggs Memorial. His other major victories came at three in the Washington Handicap at Laurel and at four in the Dixie and Saratoga Handicaps.

Star Shoot's famous son Sir Barton, who served as Man o' War's final opponent in a special $75,000 match race staged in Ontario, Canada, was also inbred to Maid of Masham. As noted in Figure 1, both Sir Barton and Star Shoot descended from her, thus creating the 'Formula One Pattern' to this exceptional family. Bred by John E. Madden and owned by Commander J.K.L. Ross, Sir Barton was best known as the first horse to win the Kentucky Derby, Preakness and Belmont Stakes, even before that trio of classics came to be known as the American Triple Crown of racing.

Sir Barton

Two other American broodmare prospects purchased with Man o' War in mind were Shady and The Nurse, both unraced, each demonstrating a similarly distinct pedigree pattern.

Bred by H.P. Whitney, Shady, a daughter of Broomstick, was a full sister to 1920 Kentucky Oaks runner-up Truly Rural. Shady's grand-dam *Sylvabelle was also the second dam of her sire, creating 'Formula One' inbreeding to the family of Broomstick. The English-bred Sylvabelle was originally imported by William Allison in 1892 for Elizabeth Daingerfield's uncle, J.R. Keene, master of Castleton Stud.

When bred to Shady, Man o' War sired three stakes winners from seven foals including the nice juvenile filly Taps, winner of the Matron and Schuylerville Stakes.

The John Madden-bred The Nurse, by Yankee, also demonstrated the 'Formula One Pattern' since her fourth dam Mannie Grey (dam of Domino) was also the second dam of her sire.

From Man o' War's first two crops, The Nurse produced a pair of bay fillies, Florence Nightingale and Edith Cavell, for the Jeffords. Both were named co-champions of their generation at age three when winning the prestigious Coaching Club American Oaks. Edith Cavell was also an exceptional older racemare with a series of important victories over males including two runnings of the Pimlico Cup.

Two more young, unraced Madden-bred broodmares sent to Man o' War during his first season at stud were Trasher, by Trap Rock, and Smoky Lamp, by Plaudit.

Trasher came from a relatively moderate family and it is possible that what made her a viable candidate for Man o' War was the strain she carried from the English sire Orme, whose dam Angelica was St. Simon's full sister. As shown in Man o' War's pedigree, St. Simon was the broodmare sire of Rock Sand, the broodmare sire of Man o' War.

Trasher produced two stakes winners for Glen Riddle when bred to Man o' War. Her daughter Maid At Arms shared three-year-old filly champion honors with Jeffords' Florence Nightingale in 1925 when she captured the Alabama Stakes and the Maryland Handicap.

The well-bred Smoky Lamp was from the immediate family of 1909 handicap champion King James as well as 1913 juvenile filly champion Southern Maid. Her sire Plaudit, like Migraine, was a half brother to Man o' War's grandsire Hastings, so their cross established inbreeding to their common dam Cinderella.

From Man o' War's small first crop, Smoky Lamp produced Lightship, whose best race for the Jeffords was her second place finish in the Alabama to Sam Riddle's Maid At Arms.

The depth in quality, particularly within Man o' War's early crops, meant that his offspring were often pitted against each other in the most important races. This was especially so, since it was rare for Riddle or the Jeffords to intentionally duck an opportunity to compete against each other at the major venues.

While Walter Jeffords was usually credited as breeder, he and his wife Sarah divided their stock to race under each's own colors. Walter's silks sported green and white stripes with green sleeves, while Mrs. Jeffords' riders wore a pink and yellow hooped jacket with pink sleeves, quite distinct from the black and yellow colors of their uncle.

Besides the close family bond, Riddle and Jeffords benefited greatly by their partnerships and cooperative purchases, especially since the two men shared a similar vision as to how Man o' War should be handled at stud.

The other side to the Riddle-Jeffords alliance was as "sparring partners." From their training center near Berlin to the major racetracks of the East Coast, both divisions continued to test each other, as they had with Man o' War and Golden Broom. It was an intense, but usually friendly, rivalry that made them both stronger.

For quite a while, Glen Riddle's best runners sired by Man o' War were typically chestnut, while the best of Red's get carrying one of the Jeffords' two sets of silks were usually bay or brown.

One race that was said to have caused Riddle to grumble at the good fortunes of his partner and kin was the 1926 Pimlico Cup when his champion three-year-old, Crusader, was upset by Jeffords' Edith Cavell thanks to a 33-pound difference in weights. Riddle's sense of racing, gleaned from thorough experience as a rider and trainer as well as an owner, was, simply, that the best horse should win.

Later, as guest of honor at the 1937 testimonial dinner of the Thoroughbred Club of America, he was quite clear on the subject:

"Now and then, a horse who can't keep up with his own shadow . . . will win over a really speedy animal, because of the unfair and unintelligent distinction in the matter of weights carried!"

Riddle and Jeffords enjoyed similar racing sensibilities and goals. Rather than emphasize brilliance and juvenile success as dictated by the H.P. Whitney Stud, their focus, like August Belmont's, was directed more toward excellence at classic distances and beyond. As a result, Man o' War's progeny were typically bred and trained with stamina in mind.

The primary races both men were looking to win were the great races of New York and the rich handicaps of Maryland, home of Glen

Riddle Farm. At Belmont Park, the main prizes were the Belmont Stakes and the Coaching Club American Oaks for three-year-old colts and fillies respectively, and, later in the season, the Jockey Club Gold Cup at two miles. At Saratoga, the two crown jewels were the Travers and the Alabama Stakes.

The gold "George III" cup, crafted by Tiffany & Co. and presented to the Riddles when Man o' War defeated Sir Barton in their 1920 match race in Canada, was donated by Mrs. Riddle to the Saratoga Association to be used as the permanent trophy for the Travers Stakes. The name of every winner of the race, beginning in 1864, is inscribed on the "Man o' War Cup" with a replica presented to the winning owner. Besides Red's victory in the Travers, Glen Riddle bred two other winners of the "Mid-Summer Classic," while the Jeffords bred and raced a total of four Travers winners.

Of course, not all of Man o' War's progeny did well for their patrons. Texas tycoon W. T. Waggoner, who could not separate Man o' War from his owner with a blank check in 1920, spent the largest amount on record for one of his offspring when going to $65,000 to collar his only yearling being offered at the 1928 Saratoga sales. The chestnut colt out of *Starflight by Sunstar, named Broadway Limited, sadly, experienced one of the worst careers imaginable.

As a two-year-old, Broadway Limited made five starts, all in major stakes races including the Futurity, but never came close to earning a check. At three, after another poor effort in the Derby Trial, he ran ninth as part of the field in the 1930 Kentucky Derby, following that up with a sixth place finish against maidens. Broadway Limited was, then, ignominiously gelded as a final measure toward getting some part of his high price tag paid back. In his first start after the operation, in the Prospect Purse for older maidens at Lincoln Fields in Illinois, he was running 11th in a 12-horse field when, coming into the stretch, he fell, and according to the track veterinarian, was probably dead before hitting the ground from heart failure. In nine starts, the poor horse never earned a dime.

For whatever reason, the sons and daughters of Man o' War who were sold publicly did not have exceptional racing careers. Of the 45 yearlings purchased at auction, at an average of $9,008, only three (seven percent) became stakes winners.

During the lavish spending of the "Roaring 20s," the few Man o' Wars available for sale generally went for huge amounts. Most of these were bred and later consigned to the Saratoga sales by Sam Riddle's friends and well-known breeders, Admiral Cary T. Grayson, Colonel Phil T. Chinn and John O. Keene. Between 1925 and 1929, the three of them sold six of Big Red's yearlings for a whopping $228,500, Chinn receiving the most for Broadway Limited.

Admiral Grayson's chestnut filly out of Tuscan Red fetched $50,500, an all-time record for a yearling in 1925. Later named War Feathers, she showed great promise in training but was injured when cast in her box and never showed her true form after that. Branded the "fifty thousand dollar lemon," she redeemed herself at stud producing four stakes winners including War Plumage, winner of the Coaching Club American Oaks at three and a national championship at age four.

After the Great Stock Market Crash in the fall of 1929, prices for Red's (and others stallions') yearlings dropped like a stone. Between 1930 and 1935, the seven of his yearlings offered for sale brought an average of $2,039.

The Thoroughbred market started to rebound in 1934, as the expansion of racing was seen as a viable new source of government revenue. Marked increases in stakes and other purses, new players from the entertainment industry and a generalized shortage of runners brought value back to the breeding game.

In 1936, Samuel Riddle decided to take advantage of the rise in prices by both reducing the size of his broodmare band, moving 15 in all, as well as offering many of his yearlings at the Saratoga summer sale. Riddle sold 32 of them for $116,700 including the sales topper, a Man o' War colt out of Bridgeen going for $18,000. Subsequently named Warbridge, he was mediocre at best.

Riddle was lucky. If he had sold his stock at Saratoga a year earlier in 1935, he probably would have lost War Admiral, a yearling colt that failed to impress his master. Riddle was probably expecting Red's next great son to be another big chestnut.

During this period, Riddle also began some breeding partnerships with his second farm manager, Harrie B. Scott. Riddle had the option to

66

buy the shared foal at a prearranged figure. Otherwise, it would be sold at the Saratoga yearling sale. Riddle had some similar pacts with his friend John Oliver Keene. Their 1937 Man o' War filly out of Silver Beauty, War Beauty, was purchased back by Keene at Saratoga for $4,200, knowing a good daughter of his mare when he saw one. She captured the rich Selima Stakes for him when particularly good at age two.

As the years went by, Riddle continued to control the size of his racing stable by selling yearlings as well as some of his established runners in training. He was not adverse to buying some well-bred yearlings at Saratoga, when so inclined. The Jeffords, on the other hand, generally raced everything they bred at Faraway, dividing the foals between them, selling some of their homebreds after their careers at the track had ended.

A good part of the racing success both Riddle and the Jeffords enjoyed was the result of engaging superior horsemen to raise and train their stock.

Man o' War's young trainer, Louis Feustel, clearly had a way with the stormy character of the Fair Play line. After parting company with Riddle, he returned to training for August Belmont II with whom he continued to do well until the Major's death in late 1924. Over that period, he trained other of Fair Play's talented offspring including Messenger, Blind Play and Ladkin, hero of the famous 1924 International Special when beating French champion Epinard. Later on, Feustel's best trainees remained rich in Fair Play blood including 1927 Horse of the Year Chance Play. Feustel, America's leading money-winning trainer in 1920 thanks to Big Red, was inducted into Racing's Hall of Fame in 1964.

Gwyn R. Tompkins succeeded Feustel and was responsible for bringing Man o' War's first two crops to the track. Glen Riddle horses were with Tompkins until the end of 1925, the year Riddle was the nation's leading money-winning owner when campaigning three champions: American Flag, Maid At Arms and Friar's Carse. Tompkins would later train for Brookmeade Stable. Riddle replaced him with his long-time foreman, George Conway.

A quiet and modest man, Conway began his apprenticeship under Matt Byrnes, trainer of Hall of Famers Firenze and Salvator in the 1880s.

Conway's first full season as Glen Riddle's head trainer was highlighted by Crusader's dominant sophomore year. He will, nevertheless, always be best remembered as the man who trained War Admiral, America's fourth Triple Crown winner. George Conway died soon after The Admiral was retired from racing in early 1939.

War Admiral and George Conway

In the early 1940s, War Relic, the last good colt Riddle campaigned, was prepared by Culton Utz who was then replaced after five starts with Walter Carter. The latter urged big wins from the bad-tempered chestnut in the rich Massachusetts Handicap and Narragansett Special when he beat Whirlaway.

Prior to Man o' War's arrival, both Riddle and the Jeffords kept their horses with W. H. Karrick, who conditioned Riddle's Yankee Witch. During the 1918 season, the two men both decided to leave that barn and begin using separate trainers.

While Big Red was with Feustel, the star-crossed Golden Broom was handled by Mike Daly. After a couple of years with him, the Jeffords experimented with a few others before choosing Robert A. Smith to train their share of the highly anticipated first runners by Man o' War. Smith had started in the August Belmont I organization in the early 1880s, galloping horses at the age of 12. At 18 and already a jockey agent, he displayed his keen eye with the remarkable purchase of Tenny, Salvator's mighty rival, for a mere $210. For the Jeffords, "Whistling Bob," as he was known, saddled the champion sisters Florence Nightingale and Edith Cavell. Later on, in the 1930s for Brookmeade Stable, Smith prepped classic winners Cavalcade and High Quest. He was inducted into the Hall of Fame in 1976.

In 1926, the Jeffords moved most of their horses in training to the barn of Scott P. Harlan. He guided their colt Mars through a rich sophomore season, even though his former barn was now calling him a "round-ankled bum!" Mars' strong campaign, combined with Scapa Flow's champion juvenile season, helped Harlan capture the U.S. trainer earnings title that year. In 1927, 1928 and 1929, Harlan was best known as the conditioner of the Jeffords' outstanding dual champion Bateau.

For much of the 1930s, the Jeffords entrusted their racing stock to Preston M. Burch who had already logged three decades of experience training stakes winners on the flat and over fences in New York, Canada, Cuba, France and Italy. Burch saddled his first winner at 17. In the 1918 Bowie Handicap, in a famous showdown of Derby winners, his George Smith beat Exterminator and Omar Khayyam. Among the very good horses he trained for the Jeffords are Firethorn and Creole Maid. Burch is also credited as the breeder of champion handicap filly Gallorette. In 1944, he gave up his public stable and began training exclusively for Brookmeade Stable. In unique fashion, Preston Burch was the son and father of Hall of Fame trainers and was himself inducted into the same honor roll in 1963. The Jeffords parted company with him in late 1938, spending the next several years in the barns of John T. Ward Jr. and W. J. "Buddy" Hirsch who later earned Hall of Fame status training stars like Gallant Bloom and Man o' War's key grandson, Intent.

The longest relationship the Jeffords family enjoyed with one trainer was with former Burch assistant Oscar White, who began developing their homebreds in the early 1940s and continued to do so for three decades. During this period, the Jeffords enjoyed their greatest and most consistent successes, including championship seasons from Pavot and Kiss Me Kate as well as co-Horse of the Year honors from One Count.

Walter Jeffords leads in his 1945
Belmont winner Pavot with Eddie Arcaro up.

This review suggests neither Riddle nor Jeffords were shy about changing trainers, no matter the perceived level of recent success. It would have been interesting to know of the real "fly on the wall" reasons for some of the break-ups.

Tomkins, Smith and Burch all went on to train for Isabel Dodge Sloane's Brookmeade Stable. Sloane, one of the original "first ladies of the American turf" and the first woman to lead the owner's ranks in earnings (doing it twice), had long kept a close eye on the combined Faraway Farm operations and was often on the lookout for new stock carrying Man o' War's blood.

One of the affairs of racing that Riddle and the Jeffords did handle quite differently was the way in which each horse should be named. The Jeffords were often very creative in their choices, playing off of the name of their mare, sometimes requiring a dictionary or encyclopedia to appreciate.

Riddle almost always gave the sons and daughters of Man o' War military-related names and he referred to them often, as their wondrous triumphs were usually his favorite topic of conversation.

Riddle's dinner partner one evening was a young woman whose racing knowledge was limited to a day or two at the course on some fashionable occasion. She listened attentively most of the evening to a recounting of the glorious performances of Man o' War's offspring.

There was a lull, and then someone from across the table asked her, "What do you think of disarmament?"

"Why, I don't know. Was he sired by Man o' War, too?"

CHAPTER FIVE

The Price of Fame

What you want is fame?
Then note the price:
All claim
To honor you must sacrifice.

Friedrich Nietzsche
German philosopher and critic of culture
1844-1900

In 1942, Man o' War, America's most famous racehorse, surpassed his own sire, Fair Play, as racing's richest stallion in terms of progeny earnings.

Now 25 years old and slowed by the infirmities of age, Man o' War was bred to a small and, what turned out to be, final set of brood-mares earlier that year. Riddle officially retired him from stud duty the following season. The prospect of adding a few more quality years of life to the great chestnut was a far better option than risking further deterioration of the stallion's health merely to secure a few more of his foals. Riddle often spoke of Man o' War as a national treasure and his retirement from stud duty was rewarded with four and one-half more years of the superstar's company.

Despite the apparent success and sentiment, no owner-breeder in the history of the American turf has ever absorbed as much public criticism for his management of a prominent stallion as did Samuel Riddle. In dozens of published accounts over the course of decades,

Riddle's handling of Man o' War's stud career has been vigorously questioned in some quarters and condemned in others.

Renowned Thoroughbred historian Abram S. Hewitt, who knew Riddle personally, saved some of his most biting remarks for the master of Glen Riddle Farm. In his 1977 book *Sire Lines* Hewitt wrote, ". . . records show that [Man o' War's] mates, by and large, were rubbish. Both their racing records and produce records were badly subnormal, and it is hard to say what Riddle was thinking of, if anything at all." Making sure nobody missed him the first time, Hewitt continued to attack in his 1982 opus, *The Great Breeders and their Methods*, when he concluded, "Riddle had one of the worst collections of mares it would have been possible to put together!"

Other analysts, both before and after Hewitt, have generally been softer in tone, but the inference has always been the same: Riddle suppressed Man o' War's brilliance at stud by keeping him virtually as a private stallion while providing him with a small, lackluster collection of broodmares that were in no way worthy of the great sire.

Kent Hollingsworth wrote in *The Blood-Horse's Silver Anniversary Edition*, "Man o' War had little or no help from his mates and credit for his high percentage of stakes winners is all his. One can only speculate what Man o' War's record would have been had he been afforded the opportunity of being mated to better mares."

Even Walter Farley's warm and fuzzy semi-fictional *Man o' War* from 1962, a book quite complimentary of Riddle as the horse's owner, questioned his subsequent mating decisions.

As a result of all of this, many internet web sites dedicated to the Man o' War saga share similar commentary, even though none of them provide any evidence to support the premise.

These opinions create a fascinating paradox. Why would Man o' War's owner, a man who once turned down a blank check for his colt, deny Big Red the best opportunities at stud? Furthermore, how much better was Man o' War expected to perform? Despite the alleged mismanagement, his stallion career was characterized, by Riddle's detractors themselves, as anywhere from superb to phenomenal. The more salient question is what precipitated all the criticisms? An exaggerated response is often more telling than the subject at hand.

For starters, it probably did not help that Sam Riddle was never the most popular horseman of his day. Seen as kind and cheerful to some, he came across as brash, even curmudgeonly, to others. Some just didn't like his "salty talk." Others, still, recalled a man who loved to offer up self-deprecatory humor while showing off his greatest prize to the throngs of Red's annual visitors to Faraway.

Actually, the racing career of Man o' War became a nerve-wracking ordeal for Riddle including death threats toward his horse and family and seemingly endless battles with an unrestrained and oftentimes ignorant or biased press. Riddle would often speak of the responsibility (burden) that came with owning Man o' War.

Table 3	MAN O' WAR'S TOP-RANKED OFFSPRING
AMERICAN FLAG	**Champion 3YO colt in 1925**
MAID AT ARMS	**Co-Champion 3YO filly in 1925**
FLORENCE NIGHTINGALE	**Co-Champion 3YO filly in 1925**
EDITH CAVELL	Ranked 2nd behind **Friar's Carse** as top 2YO filly in 1925 **Co-champion 3YO filly in 1926**
CRUSADER	**Champion 3YO colt in 1926** Ranked 3rd behind Chance Play as top older male in 1927
MARS	Ranked 6th behind Pompey as top 2YO colt in 1925 Ranked 7th behind Crusader as top 3 YO in 1926 Ranked 2nd behind Chance Play as top older male in 1927
SCAPA FLOW	**Champion 2YO colt in 1926**
FRILETTE	Ranked 4th behind Fair Star as top 2YO filly in 1926
BATEAU	Ranked 2nd behind Anita Peabody as top 2YO filly in 1927 **Co-champion 3YO filly in 1928** **Champion handicap distaffer in 1929**
GENIE	Ranked 5th behind Reigh Count as top 3YO colt in 1928
CLYDE VAN DUSEN	Ranked 4th behind High Strung as top 2YO colt in 1928 Ranked 2nd behind Blue Larkspur as top 3 YO colt in 1929
BOATSWAIN	Ranked 6th behind Burgoo King as top 3YO colt in 1932
WAR HERO	Ranked 7th behind Burgoo King as top 3YO colt in 1932

WAR GLORY	Ranked 2nd behind Head Play as top 3YO colt in 1933
WAND	Ranked 2nd behind Apogee as top 2YO filly in 1936
WAR ADMIRAL	**3YO colt champion in 1937** Ranked 2nd behind Seabiscuit as top older male in 1938 Ranked 5th behind Pompoon as top 2YO colt in 1936
WAR BEAUTY	Ranked 2nd behind Now What as top 2 YO filly in 1939
HOSTILITY	Ranked 2nd behind War Plumage as top 3YO filly in 1939
SALAMINIA	Ranked 2nd behind Fairy Chant as top 3 YO filly in 1940
DORIMAR	Ranked 2nd behind Fairy Chant as top older female in 1941
WAR RELIC	Ranked 3rd behind Whirlaway as top 3YO colt in 1941

It is also possible that some of the collective resentment directed toward Riddle was that it was not his genius that bred such an incredible animal. Hewitt recounts how at the end of WWI, Major Belmont returned from Europe and tried desperately to participate in his homebred's management, but to no avail. Man o' War was Riddle's horse.

More recently, Samuel Riddle has suffered the posthumous indignity of mischaracterization in a major motion picture when portrayed as the weak villain in the 2003 hit film *Seabiscuit*. Based on the best-selling 2001 non-fiction *Seabiscuit: An American Legend* by Laura Hillenbrand, the film's script, written by director Gary Ross, was, for 'enhanced story purposes,' nowhere near as accurate.

The casting of corpulent, clean-shaven character actor Eddie Jones, a man in his early 60s, to play the medium-built, mustachioed Riddle in his mid-70s is the first sign of inattention to accuracy. The buildup to the great match race between Charles S. Howard's Seabiscuit and Riddle's War Admiral (described in the film to be 18 hands!) portrayed the latter owner complete with dark shadows and insulting tones, ridiculing the West Coast horse while, at the same time, dodging any sort of contest with him.

Quite unsporting, actually, and completely untrue.

Hillenbrand's book, less hungry for a villain, narrates much more accurately the events leading up to the historic meeting in the $15,000 Pimlico Special, on November 1, 1938, explaining the circumstances and gamesmanship both sides took part in.

The Ross script never alluded to Seabiscuit's scheduled $100,000 match race against War Admiral, five months earlier, on Memorial Day at Belmont Park. When the Howard camp defaulted, claiming their champion's knees were bothering him, the track pleaded with Riddle, sick in bed at the time, to run his colt in the Suburban Handicap to help save their weekend of racing. But, when War Admiral's cautious trainer George Conway subsequently scratched the colt at 2 p.m. on the day of the race because of a questionable racing surface, there was hell to pay.

Esteemed turf historian John Hervey wrote, "an innocent bystander would have supposed [War Admiral's scratch from the Suburban] was an unprecedented thing and a high crime and misdemeanor on the part of Glen Riddle Stable. Though Mr. Riddle was far from the scene of action and imprisoned in a sickroom, knowing nothing of what went on until it was all over, he was subjected to the most unseemly criticism, which in some instances was even venomous in its character."

This composite photo depicts Seabiscuit and War Admiral
in their famous match race at Pimlico in 1938.

The film never mentions another scheduled engagement between the two headliners in the $50,000 Massachusetts Handicap at Suffolk Downs on June 29, 1938, which Seabiscuit also was scratched out of, this time at the very last minute. Riddle and Conway, probably petrified at that point, allowed their charge to stay in the race, despite the heavy rains. Like Seabiscuit, War Admiral was not a good mudder and ran fourth, the worst finish of his career.

Actually, going into their only meeting at Pimlico on November 1, 1938, Seabiscuit and War Admiral were eligible to meet on five different occasions and it was Seabiscuit each time that did not appear. As Hervey noted, "The Admiral was ready for the post and the older horse declined the combat."

It is always possible Hollywood filmmaker Ross was blinded by an overriding agenda, as suggested by *Philadelphia Daily News* film critic Gary Thompson, who wryly noted Sam Riddle was, "played by a portly actor going for the Lionel Barrymore award for achievement in Robber Baron villainy . . . rare restraint [was shown] in not having [him] tie a damsel to a railroad track. He was an elitist. War Admiral was an elitist. Probably a Republican. Seabiscuit was a Populist, and he filled the grandstand and infield with huddled masses yearning to breathe free . . ."

To its credit, Seabiscuit does feature some very good performances and excellent cinematography. This includes some of the most dazzling horse racing scenes in motion picture history, particularly those of Seabiscuit's heroic four-length victory over the stunned Riddle colt.

In the aftermath of the "Race of the Century," Hervey wrote, "the defeat of War Admiral by Seabiscuit was accepted by Mr. Riddle with a philosophic sportsmanship which few owners command. He offered no apologies, presented no explanation or attempt to minimize the reverse – but he did make the statement that he was ready and willing for another meeting between them."

Riddle then moved War Admiral to Narragansett Park for the Rhode Island Handicap on November 18th for which Seabiscuit was eligible, with added money of up to $25,000 if both start. War Admiral won the race eased up while Howard kept The Biscuit in Maryland, passing up the last chance they would ever have to meet again.

It seems ironic – if not unfair – that Riddle, who did his best to thwart the entry of villains, contrived or real, into the Man o' War story would, himself, be the victim of poetic license, saddled with the dark role of antagonist decades later.

Perhaps, all just part of the eternal price of fame.

CHAPTER SIX

The Man o' War Stallion Formula

"He's got everything a hoss ought to have and he's got it where a hoss ought to have it. He is de mostest hoss. Stand still, Red."

Will Harbut
Man o' War's famed groom from 1931 to 1947

Big Red's First Foals

As each of the highly anticipated first offspring sired by America's super horse was foaled, Miss Elizabeth Daingerfield announced their arrival in the pages of *The Thoroughbred Record.*

Unfortunately, things did not get off to a smooth start. The first of the get was foaled on January 27, 1922, being dead twin colts from Ursula Emma, by Broomstick. The foaling was premature, the mare not being due for almost a month.

Then the first live foal, a filly out of Masquerade by Disguise, arrived on February 26th but died very young.

Finally, the first surviving foal, a filly from the imported Bathing Girl by Spearmint arrived on February 28th. Later named Seaplane by the Jeffords, she became one of Man o' War's many important producers.

Big Red's first surviving son was By Hisself out of Colette by Collar foaled on April 18th. One of Sam Riddle's favorite stories was how the Jeffords named this first Man o' War colt.

Upon seeing Red in action for the first time, a railbird asked a nearby groom, "Who's he by?"

"He's by hisself, and there ain't nobody gonna get near him."

The brown colt went on to win stakes at both two and three, and later became a useful sire of steeplechasers.

The first of Man o' War's offspring to start in a race was Smoky Lamp's daughter Lightship. The Jeffords' filly came out at Aqueduct on July 4th, 1924, in the Astoria Stakes and faced Harry Payne Whitney's three-pronged entry of Maud Muller (eventual juvenile filly champion), Mother Goose (later winner of the Futurity and matriarch of Northern Dancer), and Swinging (dam of two-time Horse of the Year Equipoise). After showing early speed, she finished last of the four. Not surprising, given the quality of the field!

Courtesy Keeneland Library

American Flag

Man o' War's first winner was Riddle's colt American Flag, who Elizabeth Daingerfield said resembled his sire more than any other, although some would give that distinction to Crusader. American Flag won his first race, a maiden event, at Saratoga on August 6, 1924. He was the best of Red's first crop at two winning the rich Manor Handicap, and a champion at three, when unbeaten in four starts including the Withers, Belmont and Dwyer.

By midsummer in his sophomore season, however, American Flag had a problem knee to go along with chronic hoof issues that put him on the shelf for the rest of the year. This led to the following commentary from the aforementioned "Roamer" in *The Thoroughbred Record* on August 15, 1925.

"I doubt if American Flag will race again this year. This mishap is indeed unfortunate, as it is stated it was the intention of the Glen Riddle Stable to race American Flag in the Saratoga and Jockey Club Gold Cups, which would have enabled us to obtain a better line on this three-year-old's real ability. At present, he is universally conceded to be the best three-year-old out – in view of the mediocrity of his rivals, a somewhat empty honor. In reality, he is a 'Riddle' horse in more ways than one.

"Some are hopeful that (trainer) Gwyn Tompkins may be able to bring this colt around in time to meet his Jockey Club Gold Cup engagement, but this optimism does not take into consideration the cautious policy always pursued by his owners when they get hold of a horse above the ordinary. The rank and file of the race-going public has scant respect for the 'ace in a hole' policy of the Glen Riddle outfit. The average $3.85 patron of racing prefers seeing his idols racing under colors to being put in glass cases, and personally I prefer seeing a horse 'sweated for the brass' to having his spots picked for him and a paper record built up, that quickly crumbles on closer analysis."

This was just more of the diatribe aimed at the Riddle camp. Clearly American Flag was not a sound horse and the barn's careful handling of him may well have made the difference between a short but successful career and a tragic ending.

American Flag came back at age four to carry top weight in the Suburban Handicap and ran a good second to his stablemate Crusader when giving the younger Man o' War colt 20 pounds. He was retired soon thereafter.

The Target Ancestors

Man o' War's first five years at stud established him as the premiere American stallion during the second half of the 1920s.

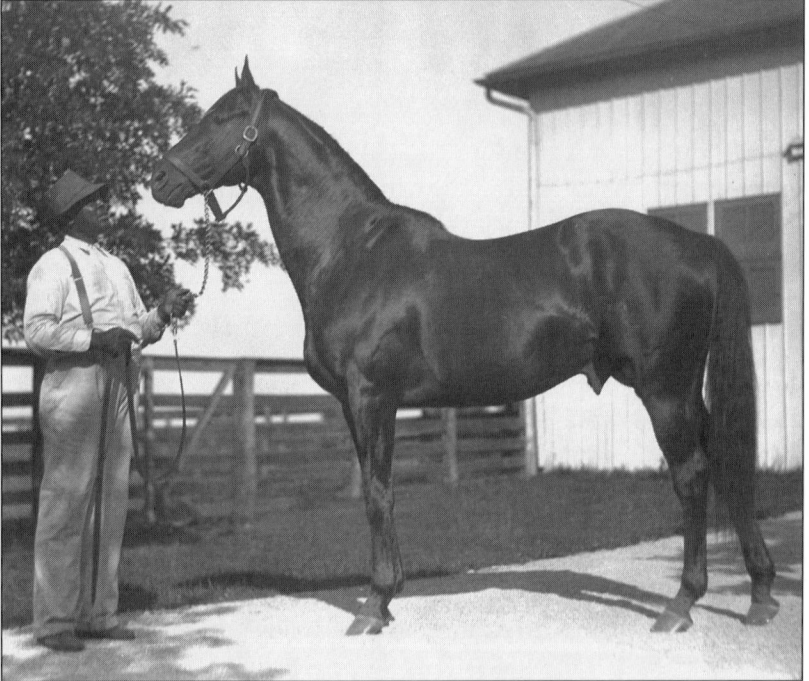

Man o' War as a young stallion.

In 1925, after Man o' War's first foals had shown their ability as two-year-olds, he was advertised with no fee stated, a practice that continued as long as he was in service. The fee, in actuality, was $5,000 thereafter, but available seasons were quite limited. Man o' War was subsequently made available, on an exclusive basis to outside mares, an average of about 10 per year, just as long as they had some of the features Faraway was looking for.

In 1926, Big Red won the U.S. sire title when sending out the best three year old (Crusader) and juvenile (Scapa Flow) of the season. His progeny's earnings that year, $408,137, was an all-time world record.

One of the consequences of this colossal start was an enduring preference toward the same profile of mate for Big Red.

Throughout Man o' War's entire sire career, his mares were generally selected on the basis of pedigree and target ancestors (inbreeding patterns), quite often at the expense of race record. This would remain true for a majority of the mares that were approved from outside breeders.

For Red's first season at stud in 1921, Riddle kept his new stallion exclusively for his and Jeffords' new collection of mares. The one exception that year was a courtesy service provided by Riddle to the outside mare Sea Name, by the obscure sire Seahorse II, who was owned by old pal James K. Maddux. This singular gift seems to support the reports that Maddux was instrumental as an advisor in Big Red's purchase.

Since much of Man o' War's pedigree was European in origin, it followed that he would blend well with the right choice of European ancestors. The most common name to appear in the pedigrees of his mares was Roi Herode, either through one of his daughters or through his best son The Tetrarch.

Of Man o' War's 381 total foals, 67 (almost 18 percent) of his progeny were out of mares carrying the blood of the grey French stallion. Fourteen (21.8 percent) of these became stakes winners. After early success with runners like American Flag and Corvette, Riddle and Jeffords continued to send Roi Herode-line mares to Man o' War and got top class performers such as the fillies Regal Lily (Alabama and Gazelle Stakes) and Wand (Matron Stakes) as well the colts Boatswain (Withers Stakes) and Soldier Song (Laurel Stakes).

Roi Herode was common in the pedigrees of Big Red's outside mares as well. The best of those offspring were the classy fillies War Beauty (Selima Stakes and Matron Handicap) and Salaminia (Alabama Stakes, later becoming the third dam of Sir Ivor) as well as the talented three-year-old colt Fairy Manhurst (Lawrence Realization).

Imported sire Star Shoot was the second most common ancestor in Man o' War's mares, appearing in the pedigrees of 60 (15.7 percent) of Red's foals. After early success with Crusader and Mars, Riddle and

Jeffords continued sending Star Shoot-line mares to Man o' War, but never got another runner nearly as good.

Outside breeders, however, bred two of Big Red's most prominent sons from Star Shoot-line mares. The gelding Clyde Van Dusen (out of a daughter of Uncle, a son of Star Shoot) is best known for his victory in the rain-soaked Kentucky Derby of 1929. A year earlier, Genie had a very good sophomore season (Dwyer S., Bowie H., 2nd Belmont S., etc.), despite being part of a particularly deep crop.

Man o' War's mares also continued to be relatively rich in the blood of the influential English sires Sundridge (son of Sainfoin's full sister Sierra) and Orme (son of St. Simon's full sister Angelica).

When famed horseman Joseph E. Widener sent an unplaced daughter of Sunstar (by Sundridge) to Man o' War he got Saratoga Handicap winner Marine. When Riddle sent an unraced daughter of Sun Briar (by Sundridge) to his stallion he bred Will Rogers Handicap winner Battle Colors.

Following early success with Maid At Arms, Man o' War continued to receive a considerable number of mares carrying the blood of Orme and subsequently sired Identify (Toboggan Handicap) and Hostility (Acorn Stakes and influential broodmare) for outside breeders. Orme could also be found in the pedigrees of prominent Riddle-breds War Hero (Travers Stakes and Saratoga Cup) and Soldier Song (Laurel Stakes).

Courtesy Keeneland Library

Orme

One of the most common American-bred ancestors in the pedigrees of Man o' War's mares was the influential sire Hamburg. His blood appeared particularly compatible since his broodmare sire, Fellowcraft, was a full brother to Man o' War's paternal great-grandsire Spendthrift. In other words, breeding Man o' War to Hamburg-line mares created inbreeding to the full brothers Spendthrift and Fellowcraft.

Courtesy Keeneland Library

Hamburg

Jeffords bred 1926 Champion juvenile colt Scapa Flow (Futurity Stakes) and later Matey (Pimlico Futurity) from mares with Hamburg in their ancestry.

One of the few broodmares sent to Man o' War from the Stud of Harry Payne Whitney was the proven producer Frillery, an unraced daughter of Broomstick out of a Hamburg mare. Their one union produced Beldame Handicap winner and influential matriarch Frillette.

Robert L. Gerry, husband of Big Red's underbidder at the yearling's famous 1918 Saratoga sale, sent a granddaughter of Hamburg to Man o' War and bred Manhattan Handicap winner Ironsides.

Another American-bred progenitor whose close relations made him an expedient cross with Man o' War was the Belmont-bred Friar Rock, Fair Play's champion half brother sired by Man o' War's broodmare sire, Rock Sand.

Friar Rock

By far, the best daughter of Friar Rock to be sent to Big Red was Riddle's Friar's Carse, consensus champion juvenile filly of 1925. The five offspring produced from the mating of Man o' War with Friar's Carse demonstrated close inbreeding [3x3] to both Rock Sand and Fairy Gold, the dam of Fair Play and Friar Rock. Riddle called the cross "an experiment in breeding." The quintet included the stakes-winning fillies Speed Boat and War Kilt, both of whom later became important matrons. It also included the very good three-year-old War Relic, who became the only son of Man o' War to carry on his tail-male line into the 21st century as great-grandsire of In Reality.

Throughout Man o' War's sire career, the composite of the pedigrees of his mates would be loaded with the blood of Roi Herode, Star Shoot, Sundridge, Orme, Hamburg, and Friar Rock. In all, more than 70 percent of Big Red's offspring carried at least one of these six target ancestors.

Table 4 is a list of Man o' War's 64 stakes winners according to lifetime earnings, including the dam, her racing status, and her sire. The table also notes any target ancestors appearing within the dam's pedigree, as well as the family number and branch (if any).

Table 4 — MAN o' WAR'S STAKES WINNERS (listed according to earnings)

Stakes Winner / Racing distinctions	Dam (race record)	Broodmare Sire	Earnings	Breeder	Target	Family #
WAR ADMIRAL br. c. 1934 / Triple Crown, 1937 Horse of Year	Brushup (up)	Sweep	$273,240	R	Snd	11-g
CRUSADER ch. c. 1923 / 1926 Horse of Year, Belmont S.	Star Fancy (up)	Star Shoot	$203,261	R	SS/M	4-m
MARS ch. c. 1923 / Travers Stakes, Dixie H., etc.	Christmas Star (SP)	Star Shoot	$128,786	J	SS	2-c
CLYDE VAN DUSEN ch. g. 1926 / Kentucky Derby, Ky Jcky Clb S.	Uncle's Lassie (SW)	Uncle	$122,402	X	SS	A4
BATEAU b. f. 1925 / co-Champion Filly at 3; Chp at 4	Escuina (p)	Ecouen	$120,760	J	FG/Eco	9-e
SCAPA FLOW b. c. 1924 / Champion 2 YO Colt, Futurity S.	Florence Webber (w)	Peep O' Day	$93,955	J	Hmb	4-m
WAR RELIC ch. c. 1938 / Massachusetts H., Kenner S.	Friars Carse (SW)	Friar Rock	$89,495	R	FR	1-o
GENIE ch. c. 1925 / Dwyer S., Bowie H., Yorktown H.	Fairy Wand (SW)	Star Shoot	$84,190	X	SS	A4
AMERICAN FLAG ch. c. 1922 / Champion 3 YO Colt, Belmont S.	Lady Comfey (u)	Roi Herode	$82,725	R	RH	7
EDITH CAVELL b. f. 1923 / co-Champion 3 YO Filly	The Nurse (u)	Yankee	$69,329	J	F#1	23-b

Stakes Winner Racing distinctions	Dam (race record)	Broodmare Sire	Earnings	Breeder	Target	Family #
WAR GLORY ch. c. 1930 Lawrence Realization S., etc.	Annette K. (up)	Harry of Hereford	$55,050	R	Snd	11-g
MARINE b. c. 1926 Saratoga H., etc.	Damaris (up)	Sunstar	$43,160	X	Snd	1-m
WAR BEAUTY ch. f. 1937 Selima S., Matron H., etc.	Silver Beauty (w)	Stefan the Great	$42,840	X	RH	3-o
WAR EAGLE ch. c. 1924 Miami Cup Handicap, Momus H.	Earine (w)	Sea Sick	$42,564	X	-	2-o
STAR SHADOW dkb/br. c. 1932 World's Fair H., Arlington Fall H.	Shady (p)	Broomstick	$39,310	R	F#1	16
SOLDIER SONG b. g. 1939 Laurel Stakes	Song (w)	Royal Minstrel	$39,230	R	RH/O	3-n
WAR HERO b. c. 1929 Travers Stakes, Saratoga Cup	Whetstone (SW)	Sweep	$38,361	R	O	1-j
IRONSIDES b. c. 1925 Edgemere H., Manhattan H., etc.	Bees Wax (w)	Celt	$37,855	X	Hmb	5-f
IDENTIFY ch. c. 1931 Governor's H., Toboggan H., etc.	Footprint (w)	Grand Parade	$36,925	X	O	1-m
SALAMINIA ch. f. 1937 Gallant Fox H., Alabama S., etc.	Alcibiades (SW)	Supremus	$36,580	X	RH	8-g
FAIRY MANHURST ch. c. 1940 Lawrence Realization	Star Fairy (up)	The Satrap	$34,212	X	RH	1-c

Name	Dam	Sire	Earnings			
BROADSIDE br. c. 1924 Independence H., Ben Ali H.	Blue Glass (u)	Prince Palatine	$32,271	X	-	4-i
MATEY ch. c. 1934 Pimlico Futurity	Tavy (w)	St. Germans	$31,750	J	Hmb	13-c
ANN ORULEY ch. f. 1932 Yankee S., etc.	Priscilla Ruley (SW)	Ambassador	$30,625	X	O	2-n
MAID AT ARMS ch. f. 1922 co-Champion 3 YO Filly	Trasher (u)	Trap Rock	$29,305	R	O	3-n
BATTLESHIP ch. c. 1927 Hall of Fame (Steeplechase)	Quarantaine (u)	Sea Sick	$29,275	X	-	10-e
SON O BATTLE b. c. 1924 Toronto Cup H., Ballston H.	Batanoea (u)	Roi Herode	$27,225	J	RH/SM	4-n
BOATSWAIN dkb/br. c. 1929 Withers S., 3rd Preakness S.	Baton (u)	Hainault	$26,650	J	RH/SM	4-n
GUN BOAT ch. g. 1922 Woodbine Steeplechase H., etc.	Star Fancy (u)	Star Shoot	$26,500	R	SS/M	4-m
ANNAPOLIS br. c. 1926 October Claiming H., etc.	Panoply (SW)	Peter Pan	$25,030	X	-	10-a
SEA FOX ch. g. 1928 Hampton Cup H., Pingree H.	Trasher (u)	Trap Rock	$25,025	R	O	3-n
ANCHORS AWEIGH br. c. 1928 Ardsley H., Autumn Days S., etc.	Good Bye (w)	Ultimus	$24,785	X	-	14-a
DORIMAR b. f. 1937 Saratoga Cup, Evening H.	Neshaminy (up)	St. James	$24,550	X	-	6-a
TAPS ch. f. 1923 Matron S., Schuylerville S.	Shady (p)	Broomstick	$24,500	R	F#1	16

Stakes Winner Racing distinctions	Dam (race record)	Broodmare Sire	Earnings	Breeder	Target	Family #
REGAL LILY ch. f. 1934 Alabama S., Gazelle S.	Regal Lady (w)	Supremus	$23,900	J	RH	8-g
DREADNAUGHT dkb/br. f. 1926 Matron S.	Crack O' Doom (w)	Ultimus	$22,425	X	-	16
INDOMITABLE dkb/br. c. 1933 W. P. Burch Memorial H.	Violet Mahoney (w)	Colin	$21,640	J	-	9-b
BY HISSELF br. c. 1922 Ardsley H., Bayview H., etc.	Colette (up)	Collar	$21,175	J	-	20
BATTLE COLORS ch. g. 1938 Will Rogers H.	Beaugingham (u)	Sun Briar	$20,925	R	Snd	4-p
BATTLESHIP GRAY gr. c. 1926 Wilson S., 2nd Laurel S.	Alice Blue Gown (w)	Luke McLuke	$20,685	X	-	11-c
WAR HAZARD ch. f. 1938 Alabama S.	Artifice (w)	Light Brigade	$20,315	R	SS	4-m
HOSTILITY b. f. 1936 Acorn S., 2nd C.C.A. Oaks	Marguerite de Valois (w)	Teddy	$19,730	X	O	16-a
JEAN BART b. c. 1933 Huron H., 3rd Preakness S.	Escuina (p)	Ecouen	$18,940	J	FG/Eco	9-e
FLORENCE NIGHTINGALE br. f. 1922 co-Champion 3 YO Filly	The Nurse (u)	Yankee	$18,650	J	F#1	23-b
U-BOAT blk. f. 1935 Worcester H.	Artifice (w)	Light Brigade	$17,460	R	SS	4-m

Name	Dam	Sire	Earnings			
HARD TACK ch. c. 1926 — Saranac H., Knickerbocker H.	Tea Biscuit (up)	Rock Sand	$16,820	X	-	9
YEDDO ch. f. 1924 — Illinois Oaks, 2nd Raceland Derby	Yokohama (SP)	Santoi	$14,608	X	-	4-k
FLEET FLAG ch. c. 1928 — Amsterdam Claiming S.	Lady Comfey (u)	Roi Herode	$14,260	R	RH	7
SHIP EXECUTIVE ch. g. 1932 — Meadow Brook Stp H., etc.	Lady Comfey (u)	Roi Herode	$14,000	R	RH	7
WAR KILT ch. f. 1943 — Demoiselle Stakes	Friars Carse (SW)	Friar Rock	$13,845	R	FR	1-o
WAND b. f. 1934 — Matron Stakes	Baton (u)	Hainault	$13,525	J	RH	4-n
ALDERSHOT ch. c. 1927 — Debut S., Fordham Claiming S.	Coronis (SW)	Voter	$13,310	X	-	10-a
VALKYR ch. f. 1925 — Richmond H., Bronxville H., etc.	Princess Palatine (u)	Prince Palatine	$13,005	X	Hmb	13-c
QUARTER DECK br. c. 1927 — Garden City Claiming S.	Trace (u)	Tracery	$12,850	X	O	1-m
FRILETTE b. f. 1924 — Beldame H., 2nd C. C. A. Oaks	Frillery (u)	Broomstick	$12,691	X	Hmb	A1
CORVETTE ch. f. 1923 — Gazelle S., 2nd Manor H., Test S.	Batanoea (u)	Roi Herode	$12,225	R	RH/SM	4-n
FULL DRESS blk. c. 1927 — Hermis H.	Shady (p)	Broomstick	$8,820	R	F#1	16
ADMIRALTY br. g. 1939 — Hendrie Stp H., etc.	Dream On (w)	Rochester	$7,065	X	-	52

Stakes Winner Racing distinctions	Dam (race record)	Broodmare Sire	Earnings	Breeder	Target	Family #
IRONCLAD ch. c. 1928 Jerome H., 2nd Toboggan H.	Violet Mahoney (w)	Colin	$6,880	J	-	9-b
SPEED BOAT ch. f. 1930 Adirondack H., Test S.	Friars Carse (SW)	Friar Rock	$6,145	R	FR	1-o
SAMMIE br. c. 1934 Huron H.	Thread (w)	Gainsborough	$5,710	X	-	8-c
WAR REGALIA ch. f. 1936 Diana H.	Regal Lady (w)	Supremus	$5,260	J	RH	8-g
KEARSARGE dkb/br. c. 1933 Miles Standish H.	Baton (u)	Hainault	$5,200	J	RH/SM	4-n
CAESARION ch. c. 1925 Champlain H.	Cleopatra (SW)	Corcyra	$4,100	X	-	3-j

Race Record:
u = unraced
up = unplaced
p = placed
w = winner
SP = stakes placed
SW = stakes winner

Target ancestors:
Snd = Sundridge
SS = Star Shoot
FR = Friar Rock
M = Migraine
FG = Fairy Gold in tail female line
SM = St. Marguerite in tail female line
F#1 = Formula One pattern mare

Hmb = Hamburg
RH = Roi Herode
O = Orme
Eco = Ecouen

Breeder:
R = bred by Riddle
J = bred by Jeffords
X = bred by outside breeders

Man o' War as a Sire

How great, then, did Man o' War become as a sire as well as an overall influence on the breed?

Table 5 is a summary of his career as a stallion. During his 22 years at stud, Big Red was never bred to more than 25 mares in any one season, resulting in an average crop size of 17.3 foals per year.

Riddle's and Jeffords' approach was that Man o' War's blood should remain precious, manifesting his influence through quality representation rather than an exaggerated number of foals.

Man o' War sired a total of 381 named foals, 64 or 16.8 percent of which became stakes winners. Nine were champions including Racing Hall of Famers War Admiral, Crusader and steeplechase hero Battleship.

Courtesy of Baltimore News American Photos, Special Collections, University of Maryland Libraries

Colt by Man o' War at Glen Riddle.

Table 5		MAN O' WAR'S CROP ANALYSIS			
Crop	Year	Number of Named Foals	Stakes Winners	# Foals out of Stakes Winners	# Foals out of Stakes Producers
1st	1922	12	5	0	2
2nd	1923	17	5	2	4
3rd	1924	23	6	2	2
4th	1925	20	5	5	2
5th	1926	18	6	4	2
1st 5 crops [ave. size 18]		90 foals	27 SWs (30%)	13 (2.6 ave.)	12 (2.4 ave.)
6th	1927	19	4	3	4
7th	1928	18	4	2	8
8th	1929	20	2	1	7
9th	1930	16	2	1	3
10th	1931	18	1	0	4
11th	1932	17	3	2	3
12th	1933	18	3	1	2
13th	1934	17	5	1	2
Middle 8 crops [ave. size 18]		143 foals	24 SWs (16.7%)	11 (1.4 ave.)	33 (4.1 ave.)
14th	1935	22	1	2	3
15th	1936	18	2	1	2
16th	1937	22	3	3	7
17th	1938	19	3	3	4
18th	1939	20	2	2	4
19th	1940	15	1	2	2
20th	1941	13	0	1	3
21st	1942	9	0	0	1
22nd	1943	10	1	1	3
last 9 crops [ave. size 16.5]		148 foals	13 SWs (8.8%)	15 (1.7 ave.)	29 (3.2 ave.)
22 crops [ave. size 17.3]		381 foals	64 SWs (16.8%)	39 (1.8 ave.)	74 (3.4 ave.)

One undeniable fact regarding Man o' War's sire career was that he was not able to maintain his tremendous early rate of siring top class runners. In his first five seasons, Big Red sired an awesome 30 percent stakes winners. In his next eight years at stud, he sired 16.7 percent stakes winners, while in his last nine years, he sired only 8.8 percent stakes winners.

Nevertheless, Table 5 suggests the drop-off was not caused by a reduction in the quality of his mares as measured by the number of stakes winners and stakes producers bred to him. Each of his crops averaged around five offspring from broodmares who were themselves stakes winners and/or proven stakes producers at the time of the breeding. Man o' War was simply unable to match the depth of his earlier crops, a very common phenomenon with many stallions.

In all, about 10 percent of Man o' War's mares were stakes winners, certainly a low figure for a sire of his caliber, while just under 20 percent had already produced a stakes winner.

Man o' War was not anywhere close to a Lexington, America's colossus of the 19th century with 16 sire titles, but such comparisons would not be really on the level, given the differences in competition the two faced in their respective eras.

Man o' War only captured one U.S. sire title, in 1926, but was second on three other occasions and, almost assuredly, would have held an advantage in progeny earnings over several of the eventual winners had he been allowed to produce a comparable number of starters. As it was, Man o' War appeared on the annual list of top 20 sires 13 different times.

In comparison, H.P. Whitney's foundation sire, Broomstick, sired about 25 percent stakes winners (from 280 total foals) while winning three sire titles and appearing on the top 20 stallion list 17 times. Man o' War was the more potent when their progeny faced each other, from the middle '20s into the early '30s, when Big Red was in his sire prime while the aging Broomstick was past his. Nevertheless, Broomstick's best offspring were probably never quite as good as Man o' War's best, despite being supported by Whitney's elite broodmare band.

Man o' War as a Broodmare Sire

Man o' War never earned a broodmare sire title and, yet, remains one of the most successful maternal grandsires in American history. His daughters produced a total of 124 stakes winners, eight of these national champions. Riddle and Jeffords bred 32 stakes winners from Red's mares, slightly more than 25 percent of the total.

Man o' War ranked second on the U.S. broodmare sire list on 10 different occasions and appeared within the top 10 a total of 22 times. During much of this period, he was overshadowed by Claiborne Farm's Sir Gallahad III (12-time leading broodmare sire) and that sire's huge perennial book of mares, resulting in an overwhelming advantage for the Claiborne stallion in the number of producing daughters.

As detailed in Table 6, if the discrepancy in opportunities between these two had not been as dramatic, Man o' War could have become the most celebrated American broodmare sire of the century instead of Sir Gallahad III.

Table 6	COMPARING SIR GALLAHAD III AND MAN O' WAR AS BROODMARE SIRES			
	*Sir Gallahad III		Man o' War	
Producing Daughters	276		177	
Foals	2,349		1,387	
Stakes Winners (/ Foals)	156	(6.6%)	124	(8.9%)
Stakes Placed (/Foals)	137	(5.8%)	93	(6.7%)
Blacktype Producers	164	(59.4%)	113	(63.8%)
Total Earnings	$29,112,121		$18,758,356	
Average Earnings per Starter	$14,593		$15,645	
Average Earnings / Start	$314		$353	
Average # Years Raced	3.96		3.76	
Average # Starts / Year	11.73		11.79	

Sir Gallahad III had almost 100 more producing daughters and almost 1,000 more maternal grandchildren than Man o' War. As a result, runners out of Sir Gallahad mares earned over $10 million more than Red's counterparts. Table 6 shows, however, that Sir Gallahad III was awarded his broodmare sire titles on sheer numbers alone. Man o' War's daughters had a higher percentage of stakes winners (8.9 percent to 6.6 percent), as well as stakes-placed runners. In other words, a significantly higher percentage of Red's daughters became the producers of black-type runners than the daughters of Sir Gallahad III (63.8 percent to 59.4 percent). For good measure, the Man o' War lot earned more on average as well.

An atypical but telling note on Man o' War's daughters at stud was that his stakes winners did not really outperform his non-stakes winners as the dams of good winners. In fact, stakes winners, winners, non-winners, and unraced mares by Red became the dams of stakes winners in about equal proportion, whereas normally good race mares collectively outperform the others as broodmares. This was due to the particularly high intrinsic value all Man o' War fillies enjoyed which, in turn, often limited their opportunities to gain black type at the track. Unless the filly exhibited the racing class early on to rank near the top of her division, it was often economically unwise, especially during the 1930s, to keep her in training. In many cases, there was only the unenviable choice of being beaten by better fillies or running in claiming races, neither much of an option for the owners of high residual stock.

One of the main reasons why Big Red's stakes-winning daughters did not collectively outproduce his non-stakes winning group is that none of the good fillies in training during the 1920s from the Jeffords barn ever had productive careers as broodmares. There is more than a suggestion that they may have received or simply ingested something that rendered them that way. Toxic compounds such as strychnine were not uncommon around some of the barns during that time period. Strychnine, for one, was said to be used both as rat poison and as a performance enhancer on race day.

Champion Edith Cavell delivered one live foal (of moderate ability) along with four dead ones. Her older champion sister Florence Nightingale could only throw three live foals, none who could run, while two-time champion Bateau was completely infertile. It's actually quite remarkable that Jeffords would become as successful a breeder as he did having not gotten any support at stud from these three matriarchal prospects.

Where's the Beef?

Was there ever a legitimate basis to believe that Man o' War was mismanaged at stud?

Not really, particularly after Big Red eclipsed his own great sire, Fair Play, in 1942 for the all-time record in total progeny earnings. The criticisms, nevertheless, continued and seemed to revolve around three key issues: 1) the smallish size of Man o' War's annual book of mares, 2) the accusations that he was maintained as virtually a private stallion, and 3) the allegations that the broodmares chosen for Red were usually not worthy.

Regarding the number of mares covered each year by Man o' War, it is true that if his book was somewhat larger Big Red probably would have landed more sire and broodmare sire titles. Nevertheless, Man o' War's annual crop average of 17.3 foals was actually higher than the standard for many important sires of his time period. Whitney's Broomstick averaged only 11 foals per year. Belmont's Fair Play only averaged about 13. Star Shoot and Sir Gallahad III were at the high end, averaging about 28 and 24 foals per year, respectively. Not surprisingly, the latter two with the larger books and greater commercial interests had lower lifetime rates of siring stakes winners.

The argument that Riddle and Jeffords monopolized Man o' War throughout his stallion career is also, for the most part, unjustified. Table 4 indicates that 27 (42 percent) of Big Red's stakes winners were, in fact, bred by outside breeders. This also approximates the share of Man o' War's total progeny bred by outside breeders during his prime. A comparable 46 percent of the stakes winners sired by H.P. Whitney's Broomstick were bred by outside breeders, and never a murmur of protest.

In a detailed article from late 1937 in *The New Yorker* magazine, Riddle acknowledged that several times he waived the hefty stud fees when he thought some particularly good result might come from breeding Man o' War to a specific mare, especially if the breeder could not afford the steep fee. Big Red's team obviously had a list of specific features they were looking for.

One early example of this was the mutual donations of stallion and mare services in 1922 by Riddle and Arthur B. Hancock Sr., respectively, with the hope that the resultant colt would ultimately serve at stud at the Federal Stud at Front Royal, Virginia, for the U.S. Army Remount Service, a cause particularly close to the heart of Major Belmont. The mare chosen, Star Puss by Jim Gaffney, happened to be a granddaughter of *Golden Garter, an obscure half-brother to Sainfoin, while her third dam was by Star Shoot.

Instead of a colt, the Service was rewarded with a filly that was sold for its benefit at the 1924 Saratoga yearling sale for $8,000. The brown daughter of Man o' War, subsequently named Siren, was conditioned by former Belmont trainer Sam Hildreth who found her to be one of the few horses he had ever seen who was much better on wet race-tracks. Retired after three wins from six starts, she became the dam of Juvenile Stakes winner Black Buddy.

In a later instance, Sam Riddle presented a complimentary Man o' War season in 1938 to the wife of a friend, Silas Mason, who operated Duntreath Farm in Lexington and had recently died. The mare sent to Faraway, Mid Victorian, was by Preakness winner Victorian whose third dam Slippers was a half-sister to Hastings, Man o' War's grandsire. Victorian was the primary stallion at Duntreath. The resultant foal, Maidoduntreath, was never raced but ultimately became the dam of three stakes winners including a Hollywood Oaks winner, later the granddam of Kelso, immortal recipient of an unprecedented five consecutive Horse of the Year awards (1960-1964).

Given the circumstances, it is certainly possible that some of the waves of criticism towards Riddle came from outraged breeders whose mares were rejected. Sour grapes? Maybe.

The fact is many of Kentucky's top breeders did send mares to Man o' War, often times getting exceptional runners. The distinguished list included Harry Payne Whitney, William Woodward, Mereworth Farm, and Shandon Farm as well as Greentree Stud and Wheatley Stable.

Ironically, August Belmont II – the man who bred Man o' War only to lose him in a rush of patriotism – became one of his first outside breeders in 1924. Two of Big Red's future stakes winners, Broadside and Yeddo, were foaled at his Nursery Stud only months before the great horseman's death.

In regard to the notion that Man o' War suffered from mares that were "rubbish," perhaps the results should just speak for themselves.

The broodmares Allison selected for Man o' War were comparable to the ones he purchased at Newmarket almost 30 years earlier that helped initiate the dominant Castleton dynasty. Both groups were characterized by promising pedigrees at the expense of racing performance.

Admittedly, the aggregate race record of Man o' War's broodmares was somewhere between nonexistent and inconsistent. But should racing ability in the mare always be the primary criterion?

As conventional breeding theory would anticipate, Table 7 verifies that Man o' War did significantly better with broodmares who were stakes winners (28 percent SWs) and stakes producers (25.5 percent SWs). Just the same, the data goes on to show that the most important factor in enhancing Man o' War's rate of siring stakes winners was the presence of the aforementioned target ancestors in his mares. Man o' War's progeny out of stakes-winning and/or stakes-producing broodmares without any of these pedigree ingredients were actually quite unremarkable as a lot.

Table 7   MAN O' WAR WITH BROODMARES WHO WERE STAKES WINNERS AND/OR STAKES PRODUCERS, WITH OR WITHOUT TARGET ANCESTORS

	Number mares	Number foals	SWs (%)	With target ancestors / SWs(%)	No target ancestors / SWs(%)
Stakes winners (SWs)	26	39	11 (28%)	22/8 (36%)	17/3 (17.5%)
Stakes producers (SPs)	38	74	19 (25.5%)	58/17 (29%)	16/2 (12.5%)
Both stakes winner and producer	6	8	4 (50%)	6/4 (67%)	2/0 (0%)

It is also worth noting that the same target ancestors who did best with Man o' War were also very prominent in the dams of the best off-spring of other important stallions demonstrating the Fair Play - Rock Sand cross (Table 2) at other farms.

Most of the dams of Chance Shot's best and richest offspring carried strains of Roi Herode in their pedigrees including the dam of Belmont Stakes winner Peace Chance and distaff champion Fairy Chant. The dam of Chance Play's best offspring, Pot o' Luck, was out of a Hamburg mare. So, too, was the dam of My Play's richest offspring, Plucky Play. Nine of Mad Hatter's 22 stakes winners were out of mares with the blood of Hamburg, while the dam of Mad Hatter's best and richest daughter, Snowflake, was out of a Roi Herode mare.

As Chapter 7 describes, these trends also continued for most of Man o' War's sons.

Was there anything Man o' War failed to accomplish? Only that he never 'reproduced' himself, if that could even have been possible. As such, it would seem he could never be credited as great a stallion as he was a racehorse.

To resolve the 'catch-22,' Sir Charles Leicester simply concluded in his 1957 book *Bloodstock Breeding* that "coupling [Man o' War's] racing ability with his success as a stallion he must be regarded as near the best and possibly actually the best horse bred in America in this century."

As it stands, over 24 percent of Big Red's sons became stakes winners while more than 48 percent of his daughters became stakes winners and/or the dams of stakes winners. Numbers like those would normally shield a horseman from censure. Instead, a small modern myth developed.

In the case of the normally brilliant turf historian Abram Hewitt, he admitted in his books that Big Red "was the first great horse the author ever saw perform" and that August Belmont II was not at all a stranger in the Hewitt home as he was growing up. It is, therefore, not much of a stretch to see how the impressionable young fan could have gotten carried away when it came to the prodigal Man o' War, his inordinately fortunate new owner and Major Belmont whose best horse had gotten away.

The fact that Riddle engaged someone closely associated with the dreaded Figure System to help in shaping Man o' War's second career only added to Hewitt's cynicism, referring to Allison as "Lowe's high priest of England." This was not meant as a compliment. As Table 4 shows, however, 22 – or more than one-third – of Man o' War's stakes winners were from so-called non-preferential families, making it very unlikely the Figure System was ever adhered to by anyone on Man o' War's breeding team.

Actually, there was a well-known owner-breeder who did manage his stallion in exactly the manner Sam Riddle was accused, but without any of the reproach.

The popular Charles S. Howard retired Seabiscuit after his victory in the 1940 Santa Anita Handicap as the richest Thoroughbred in history. Instead of buying or finding his big horse a well-located farm where he could benefit from a decent book of mares, Howard returned "The Biscuit" to his beloved Ridgewood Ranch near Willits, California, in the remote redwood country about 150 miles north of San Francisco. There he was bred, almost entirely, to Howard's eclectic band of brood-mares, most of them recently imported from Europe and Argentina, usually without any blood complementary to Seabiscuit's. Ridgewood, at the time, was more than 600 miles away from the nearest major breeding farm and virtually no breeders were willing to subject their stock to the rigorous haul.

The laid-back Seabiscuit was by Man o' War's irascible son Hard Tack. His dam, Swing On, a daughter of Whisk Broom II, was from the elite yards of H.P. Whitney. Seabiscuit's rags-to-riches career may have lowered expectations of him as a sire, but yet, he actually came from a much better family of runners and sires than either Man o' War or War Admiral. His close relative and two-time Horse of the Year Equipoise would become America's leading sire in 1942.

Seabiscuit's nine years at stud yielded only 108 foals, many that won (61 percent) but few with much class (four SWs). Fittingly, the Howard mare (Illeanna by Polymelian) Seabiscuit did do best with, producing his best son and daughter, was from the family of Whisk Broom II, his broodmare sire.

Over time, Seabiscuit's influence on contemporary pedigrees has become negligible and one cannot help but think if this was the work of "Old Man" Riddle, instead of the media-savvy Charles Howard, "Roamer" and Hewitt would have truly had a field day.

CHAPTER SEVEN

The Spread of Man o' War's Blood

Hold your strength till the barriers fly,
then close with the leaders eye to eye.
Thundering hooves and the mad jammed race,
blood in the nostrils, sweat in the face.
And children, remember wherever you are,
you carry the blood of Man o' War.

Anonymous

THE FARAWAY STALLIONS

Man o' War and his old sparring partner, Golden Broom, entered stud together in 1921 at Elizabeth Daingerfield's leased Hinata facility. On May 22, 1922, these two five-year-old chestnut stallions, followed by their first sucklings, their dams and others among a growing collection of broodmares, traveled the short distance to Riddle and Jeffords' new Faraway Farm, or Faraway Stud as it was first known.

The Jeffords' Golden Broom never really stayed sound long enough to confirm his record Saratoga yearling price. He developed a quarter crack after winning the Saratoga Special, his only lifetime win. In his next start, the infamous Sanford Memorial of 1919, he weakened in the stretch and unwittingly set a trap for Man o' War leading to Red's one and only loss. After that debacle, Golden Broom's bad feet prevented him from returning to his earlier form.

At Faraway, Golden Broom enjoyed a fair career at stud [127 foals; 12 SWs (nine percent)]. He was tried with many of the same mares bred to Man o' War but rarely with as good a result.

Golden Broom wins the 1919 Saratoga Special.

Most of Golden Broom's best offspring demonstrated female family inbreeding patterns involving his broodmare sire, Hamburg. His richest son, the multiple stakes-winning sprinter Polydor, was inbred 5x5 to Mannie Gray, the dam of Domino and the grand dam of Hamburg.

As previously described, Hamburg represented one of Man o' War's target ancestors, since his broodmare sire, Fellowcraft, was a full brother to Spendthrift, Red's great grandsire. This made Golden Broom a viable stallion option for some of the early daughters of Man o' War as they became available. The best individual from this cross was the Riddle-bred Gold Foam who captured the 1935 Travers Stakes.

Golden Broom's stallion stats probably make him appear better than he actually was. Next to Big Red, he was probably afforded the best selection of broodmares at Faraway, better than the books of the sons of Man o' War that he was soon competing against. His influence on the breed would, nevertheless, soon become negligible.

Over the next few years, several more stallion prospects were brought to Faraway Farm. All three were horses that were purchased as young racing prospects by Riddle and Jeffords and had completed stakes winning careers for them. Unfortunately, none brought very much good to the program. They were all of sire lines that would soon completely fade out.

Star Hampton, a son of Star Shoot who won a couple of stakes for the Jeffords, entered stud in 1922. His record at stud [45 foals; one SW (two percent)] earned him an early pension from duty.

Oceanic, another Madden-bred, was a son of The Finn from the family of Sweep. He entered stud in 1925, was given a few opportunities with a few of Riddle's proven mares and then retired after little success.

Big Blaze, by Campfire, was a pleasing yearling purchase for Sam Riddle, winning a number of important stakes for his owner while he was eagerly awaiting Red's first foals' arrival at the track. He entered stud at Faraway in 1927 and then sired 1931 juvenile champion Burning Blaze in his second season. Despite this one instance of brilliance with an outside mare, Big Blaze [131 foals; five SWs (four percent)] never sired another nearly as good and was ultimately deemed a failure as a sire of runners and relegated as an Army remount stallion.

The next wave of new stallion blood added to the Faraway roster consisted of four of Man o' War's best sons, all bred and raced by Riddle or the Jeffords during Red's early years at stud.

In 1927, Sam Riddle's American Flag became Big Red's first son to join him at stud. Granted the stall in the spacious stallion barn next to his legendary sire, his initial stud fee was $1,500.

After touring Faraway Farm that summer, Neil Newman ("Roamer") wrote, "I was not greatly impressed with Man o' War's son American Flag – his future as a sire, naturally, is on the knees of the gods, but I shall be greatly surprised if he makes the grade."

American Flag was probably the scion who suffered most from the competition for mares with Man o' War, Golden Broom and the other Faraway stallions. Never particularly well supported by either Riddle or Jeffords, he did his best work with outside mares. Breeders unable to send their mares to Man o' War instead often bred them to American Flag [183 foals; 16 SWs (nine percent)].

Like his sire, American Flag did best with broodmares whose pedigree demonstrated one or more of the aforementioned target ancestors. Star Shoot was, by far, the most common ingredient in the dams' pedigrees of his best runners. His best and richest son Gusto

($151,655) was out of a Star Shoot mare. Gusto was among the best three-year-olds of 1932 when taking the American Derby, the rich Classic Stakes as well as the Jockey Club Gold Cup against his elders. He was, unfortunately, later destroyed while still in training.

American Flag's best daughter was Nellie Flag ($59,665; Selima and Matron Stakes, etc.). For her breeders at Calumet Farm, she became the first in a long line of champions when picking up juvenile filly honors in 1934. Nellie Flag would later initiate one of Calumet's most celebrated families, serving ultimately as the matriarch to champions such as Forego and Bold Forbes. What also seems particularly interesting is that Nellie Flag was a member of the family of Fair Play (see Figure 1).

Another extremely important American Flag mare was Lady Glory who became the grand dam of Raise A Native, sire of Mr. Prospector and Alydar. Given the magnitude of these bloodline icons, the modern racehorse would have been shaped a lot differently without Lady Glory.

In early 1942, shortly after America's entry into World War II, Riddle presented the 20-year-old stallion to the U.S. Remount Service in Virginia where he died later that year.

American Flag appeared in the top 20 on the annual U.S. sires rankings twice, in 1932 and 1934, outranking Man o' War both years. Despite his limitations at stud, American Flag still became an effective sire whose name will always be enshrined within contemporary pedigrees through these two daughters of his.

Newman, who was right a lot and wrong a lot, got this one wrong.

The second son of Red to arrive at Faraway was Mars in 1928. Almost a full hand shorter than his sire, Mars and his initial stud fee of $2,000 were never in favor with outside breeders. All four of his stakes winners were bred by Walter Jeffords. The best of these was the brown gelding Thursday who won back-to-back runnings of the prestigious Riggs Handicap at Pimlico. His granddam was by the target ancestor Hamburg.

Despite Thursday's victories, Mars [87 foals; four SWs (five percent)] would soon be deemed mediocre as a stallion and was used sparingly after that. The otherwise popular Jeffords-bred died in 1949 at the age of 26, his remains buried at Faraway Farm.

Crusader, one of Man o' War's two greatest sons on the racetrack, was one of his sire's biggest disappointments at stud. Originally leased by Riddle to Col. Phil T. Chinn's Himyar Stud in 1929, Crusader was returned a year later when Chinn declared bankruptcy. Back at Faraway with a fee of $1,500, Crusader [120 foals; six SWs (five percent)] failed to impress. The best of his progeny, Royal Crusader, won the 1941 Del Mar Handicap, having run second in the Santa Anita Derby the year before. This one's dam was closely inbred to Hamburg.

In 1938, Riddle leased Crusader to Rancho Casitas in Ventura, California, where he died a couple of years later. His blood survives to this day through his best producing daughter Heatherland, matriarch of Preakness winner Candy Spots as well as Hollywood Gold Cup winners Correspondent and Prove It.

The star-crossed Boatswain found things just as difficult when he returned to Faraway in 1933. Given very few chances with Riddle and Jeffords mares, Boatswain [123 foals; six SWs (five percent)] failed to excite outside breeders as well. He was soon moved on to H.P. Headley's Beaumont Farm before being banished to Cuba where he did, at least, sire a local Derby winner.

In October of 1930, Miss Elizabeth Daingerfield retired as manager of Faraway. She was replaced by Harrie B. Scott, who was well known for skillfully operating several important farms including Glen Helen Stud where Riddle had kept his small band of broodmares before establishing Faraway.

John Buckner stayed on for a few additional months while the new management was getting settled, and then followed Miss Daingerfield back to Haylands, relinquishing Man o' War to the groom who in subsequent years came to be the one most closely associated with him, Will Harbut.

More of a spokesman than a groom, Harbut became the most famous tour guide in America. He would often describe himself as having the greatest job in the world. Harbut's lavish orations on Man o' War's countless achievements thrilled the daily flock of visitors to Faraway and made him as much an attraction as the great horse they had come to see.

Man o' War and Will Harbut

Harbut adored Big Red and followed Mr. Riddle's instructions to a T. Instructed by his boss that visiting hours should end at four, Harbut did not interpret it to mean 4:01. While visiting Faraway, Riddle would sometimes make a special exception to this, but not Harbut. The wife of the Secretary of the United States Treasury once arrived at the farm gates five minutes late and, despite her pleas to see the famous horse, was refused admission by his steadfast groom.

When in the presence of Man o' War, there were two basic rules: 1) No touching and 2) No pictures.

The "no touching" policy probably dates back to Red's appearance at the Rose Tree Hunt Club when frenzied souvenir hunters had their way with him and poor Riddle almost lost his mind. The "no pictures" policy was, simply, a way of avoiding the circulation of unflattering photographs taken by amateurs. It also, probably, stimulated the sale of the official postcards of the perfectly posed Big Red in all his glory.

OUTSIDE STALLIONS

By the early 1930s, the Riddle and Jeffords broodmare bands included a growing number of Man o' War's daughters. The inadequate returns with Golden Broom and the other non-Man o' War-line stallions at Faraway necessitated judicious decisions as to the best outside stallion blood to be introduced. The selections made over the course of the next few decades were an eclectic blend of proven and prominent stallions, top prospects as well as some who could be only considered obscure.

What the large majority of these sires had in common were their pedigrees which featured one or more of the aforementioned target ancestors to Man o' War and/or other key individuals who created important female family inbreeding patterns in the resultant offspring.

Another characteristic of the outside stallions chosen for Faraway's mares was that they were typically beyond their first couple of seasons of stud duty. Satisfaction with the looks of an outside candidate's early progeny, it would seem, was a priority before any new sire commission.

One of the first and most effective outside lines tested by Jeffords was the male line of Sundridge, one of Man o' War's target ancestors. The first exceptional horse bred by Jeffords that was sired by an outside stallion was the 1932 brown colt Firethorn by the Sundridge stallion Sun Briar.

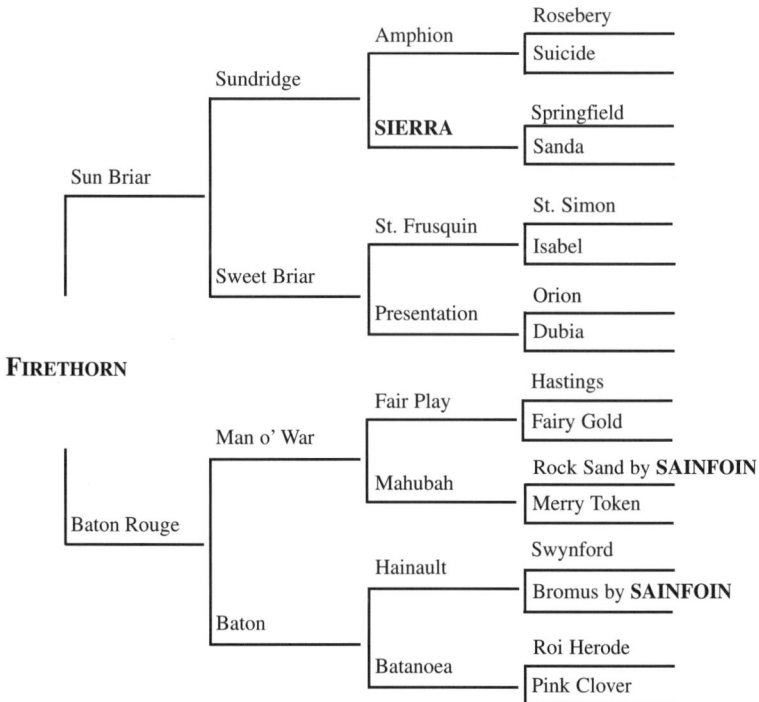

FIRETHORN pedigree chart:

- **Sun Briar**
  - **Sundridge**
    - **Amphion**
      - Rosebery
      - Suicide
    - **SIERRA**
      - Springfield
      - Sanda
  - **Sweet Briar**
    - **St. Frusquin**
      - St. Simon
      - Isabel
    - **Presentation**
      - Orion
      - Dubia
- **Baton Rouge**
  - **Man o' War**
    - **Fair Play**
      - Hastings
      - Fairy Gold
    - **Mahubah**
      - Rock Sand by **SAINFOIN**
      - Merry Token
  - **Baton**
    - **Hainault**
      - Swynford
      - Bromus by **SAINFOIN**
    - **Batanoea**
      - Roi Herode
      - Pink Clover

113

This mating may have been influenced, if not inspired, by America's best handicap horse at the time, earnings record holder Sun Beau (champion in 1929, 1930 and 1931). He was by Sun Briar and his dam was an unraced daughter of Fair Play out of a Rock Sand mare. As a result, his pedigree featured a 4x4 cross to the full siblings Sierra and her brother Sainfoin.

In Firethorn's case, Jeffords bred Sun Briar to a Man o' War mare (Boatswain's full sister) who was inbred to Sainfoin, creating a 3x5x5 sister-brother pattern.

Firethorn's racing career was hindered both by injury and being of the same generation as 1935 Triple Crown winner Omaha, running second to him in the Preakness and Belmont. He nevertheless became the winner of a number of important events including a dramatic nose victory over Granville in the Suburban at age four and the Jockey Club Gold Cup at both three and five. John Hervey wrote of Firethorn, "he could go both far and fast and when he was at his best he was capable of splendid things."

Another Sundridge-line stallion that Walter Jeffords did particularly well with was 1943 Triple Crown winner Count Fleet. Dispatching several of his daughters and granddaughters of Man o' War to the court of Count Fleet in the late '40s and early '50s, Jeffords was rewarded with the champions One Count and Kiss Me Kate.

One Count was named 1951 co-Horse of the Year at the age of three when he beat his peers in the Belmont and Travers Stakes and then older horses in the Jockey Club and Empire City Gold Cups.

Kiss Me Kate was honored as champion three-year-old filly of 1952 when she captured the Acorn and Alabama Stakes as well as the Delaware Oaks. At four and five, she added the New Castle and Firenze Handicaps.

This cross of Count Fleet with daughters and granddaughters of Man o' War also generated C.V. Whitney's 1952 Horse of the Year, Counterpoint, as well as a good number of other important representatives by their sire. Moreover, the development of the Sundridge line in America was in large part dependent upon Sainfoin blood and the resultant sister-brother cross of Sierra and Sainfoin.

Another imported male line that flourished in mid-20th century America was that of foundation sire *Teddy whose paternal great-grand-sire Orme was one of Man o' War's target ancestors. Riddle and Jeffords started sending Man o' War mares to the sons of Teddy in the early 1940s. In 1941, they both bred good stakes winners by the Teddy stallion Bull Dog who stood at Coldstream Stud. Rodney Stone, bred by Riddle and sold as a yearling for $5,100, won the Sanford Stakes (the only race his broodmare sire ever lost), while Jeffords bred and raced Westminster who captured the Narragansett Special. Later on, the reverse of the cross, Man o' War's son War Admiral with the daughters of Bull Dog, also proved productive.

Another of Walter Jeffords' sage mating decisions, around that same time, was his choice of Teddy's son Case Ace for a quintet of Man o' War's daughters he had decided to remove from training. Instead of shipping them direct from Glen Riddle Farm in Maryland to Faraway Farm in Kentucky, he sent them first to Joseph Roebling's Harmony Hollow Farm in New Jersey to be bred to Case Ace, whose pedigree, interestingly, featured descendancy from the family of Roi Herode and Bend Or.

All five of the resultant 1942 foals became winners, three were stakes winners. One of the three fillies was Ace Card who won the Schuylerville Stakes at two and the Gazelle Handicap at three. She was named Broodmare of the Year in 1952 when her son One Count won co-Horse of the Year honors.

One of the two Case Ace colts turned out to be even more brilliant. This was Pavot. Undefeated in eight starts as juvenile champion, he followed up with huge wins in the Belmont Stakes at three and the Jockey Club Gold Cup at four.

These marvelous results achieved by the Jeffords camp convinced Case Ace's owner Joseph Roebling to attempt in recreating the benefits of this pattern, in reverse, by breeding his Case Ace mare Carillon to Man o' War's best son, War Admiral. The subsequent offspring included 1948 juvenile champion Blue Peter and his winning sister Portage, who went on to forge her own important clan, one that included Roebling's 1994 Broodmare of the Year Fall Aspen and all of her successes.

Man o' War mares also did well with the Teddy-line stallion Roman. In all, he sired a total of eight stakes winners out of Red's mares including West Coast black type earner The Shaker, bred by Samuel Riddle.

The Hyperion stallion Heliopolis, also standing at Coldstream Stud, combined with Man o' War's daughters to sire seven stakes winners including the good sprinter Red Harrigan (Carter H., etc.), bred by Riddle and foaled several months after his death. Heliopolis was also the sire of Ace Admiral (Travers S., etc.), Helioscope (Suburban H., etc.) and Brookmeade Stable's Greek Ship (Metropolitan H., etc.), all three the issue of former Riddle mares.

The male line of Phalaris was first imported to America in the late 1920s and has become increasingly dominant ever since. Two representatives of the Phalaris line which Walter Jeffords did particularly well with were *Pharamond II and his son Menow who both stood at Hal Price Headley's Beaumont Farm.

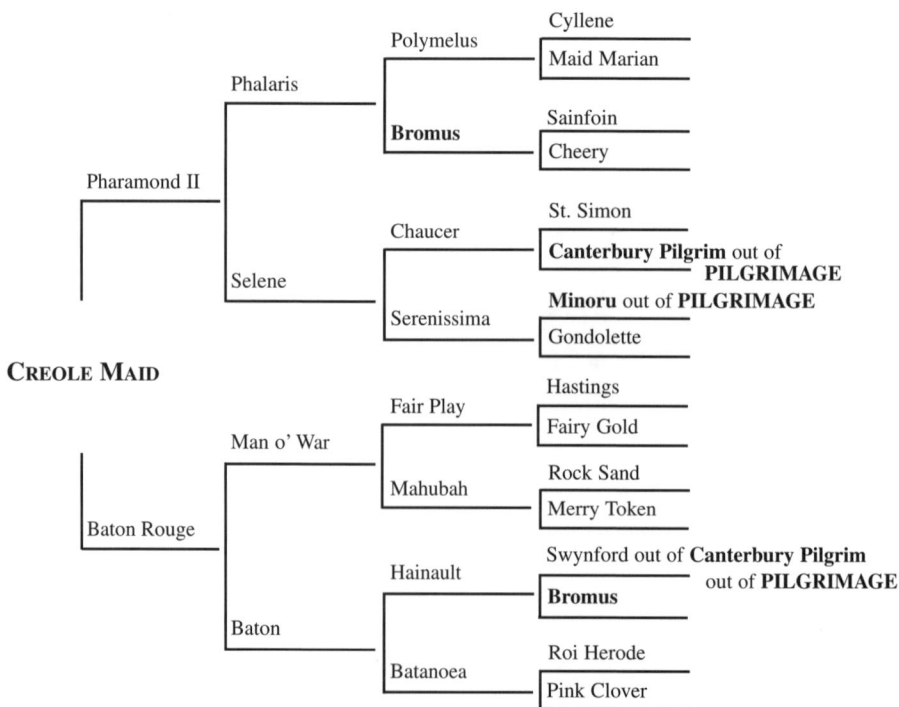

CREOLE MAID

- Pharamond II
  - Phalaris
    - Polymelus
      - Cyllene
      - Maid Marian
    - **Bromus**
      - Sainfoin
      - Cheery
  - Selene
    - Chaucer
      - St. Simon
      - **Canterbury Pilgrim** out of **PILGRIMAGE**
    - Serenissima
      - **Minoru** out of **PILGRIMAGE**
      - Gondolette
- Baton Rouge
  - Man o' War
    - Fair Play
      - Hastings
      - Fairy Gold
    - Mahubah
      - Rock Sand
      - Merry Token
  - Baton
    - Hainault
      - Swynford out of **Canterbury Pilgrim** out of **PILGRIMAGE**
      - **Bromus**
    - Batanoea
      - Roi Herode
      - Pink Clover

Jeffords sent Firethorn's dam, Baton Rouge, to Pharamond II and got Creole Maid, one of the best of her generation at two and three when winning the Adirondack and Schuylerville Stakes and then the Coaching Club American Oaks by four lengths over year-end champion Handcuff.

In this brilliant mating, Jeffords was crossing complementary strains of two different families. Baton Rouge's broodmare sire, Hainault, was a half-brother to Phalaris while his sire, Swynford, was a half-brother to Pharamond's broodmare sire, Chaucer.

Pharamond's son Menow, a champion at two, was out of Alcibiades (Supremus-Regal Roman by Roi Herode). When bred to Man o' War Alcibiades produced 1940 Alabama Stakes heroine Salaminia for her breeder H.P. Headley. It was now up to Walter Jeffords to attempt a reversal of this cross by sending a daughter of Man o' War to Menow.

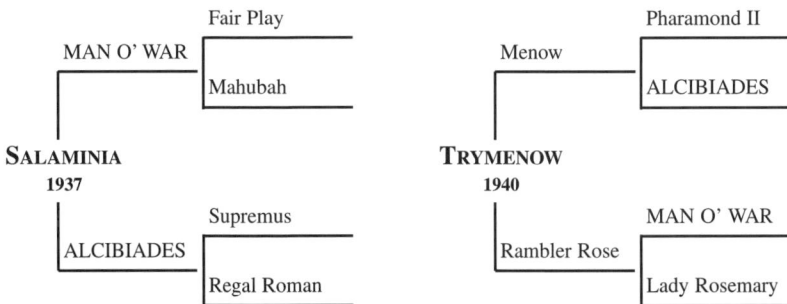

	Fair Play		Pharamond II
MAN O' WAR		Menow	
	Mahubah		ALCIBIADES
SALAMINIA		**TRYMENOW**	
1937		1940	
	Supremus		MAN O' WAR
ALCIBIADES		Rambler Rose	
	Regal Roman		Lady Rosemary

The mare Jeffords sent, Rambler Rose, was of a Swynford broodmare sire line thereby also creating inbreeding to Canterbury Pilgrim in the process. In 1942, Rambler Rose foaled the Menow colt Trymenow who became a multiple stakes winner and was best known for beating his more famous stablemate Pavot as well as Racing Hall of Famer Stymie in the 1945 Whitney Stakes.

Red's daughters also did well with Pharamond's full brother *Sickle, producing eight stakes winners with him. Riddle bred one of these, but the two best were Jabot (Selima Stakes, etc.) and her younger brother Cravat (Hollywood Gold Cup, etc.) out of the Man o' War mare Frilette, owned by C.V. Whitney.

Faraway broodmares often clicked with stallions from the farm of Cornelius Vanderbilt Whitney who for six decades carried on with distinction the breeding and racing legacies of his famous father, Harry Payne Whitney, and grandfather, William Collins Whitney.

In 1937 Riddle sent his stakes-winning mare Speed Boat to Whitney's Equipoise, a two-time Horse of the Year, and got Level Best. Purchased by Crispin Oglebay at the Saratoga yearling sales for $7,600, she became the top-ranked juvenile filly of 1940 when taking eight of 11 starts against both sexes. Her best race at age three was a wire-to-wire victory in the 1 3/8 mile Coaching Club American Oaks.

The same season Riddle sent Speed Boat to Equipoise, Whitney dispatched Racing Hall of Famer Top Flight to Faraway for an appointment with Man o' War. The newspapers referred to the union as "the mating of the ages" and it did certainly look that way on paper. Top Flight carried the blood of Hamburg and her fourth dam was a full sister to Whitney's father's famed Whisk Broom II. The black colt with the majestic name of Sky Raider won his first two races but, sadly, injured himself in his third, never to compete again.

In 1941, C.V. Whitney imported his most successful sire, *Mahmoud, from England where he had won the Derby in record time. The grey stallion's legendary granddam, Mumtaz Mahal, "the flying filly," was a granddaughter of Roi Herode and Sundridge, two of Red's target ancestors, suggesting his compatibility with Faraway stock.

In all, seven of Mahmoud's 70 stakes winners were bred by the Faraway team including the outstanding racing fillies Snow Goose and Adile, bred and owned by the Jeffords.

In 1947 Snow Goose beat famed distaff champion Gallorette in both the Beldame Stakes and Ladies Handicap as a three-year-old and then came back to beat the boys in the Saratoga Cup at four.

Adile was best at three when she won the Alabama Stakes, the Monmouth Oaks and the Empire City Gold Cup against older males. It was a campaign that could have earned a championship for a sophomore filly in most years, but not 1949 when vying with the likes of the Calumet Farm duo Wistful and Two Lea.

When Firethorn, the first grandson of Man o' War with sire potential, was retired at the end of the 1937 season, there was little that could be done with him at Faraway. Neither Riddle nor Jeffords were keen, up to that point, on practicing close inbreeding to Man o' War.

C.V. Whitney, on the other hand, saw Firethorn as possessing the combination of speed, stamina and pedigree that he was looking for. As a result, Jeffords sold a half interest in the Sun Briar stallion to Whitney for service at his farm. In the mid-40s, Whitney sent Firethorn along with his Broomstick stallion, Halcyon, to Faraway Farm for several seasons.

Walter Jeffords, who bred Firethorn's best son Post Card in 1947, may have been influenced by the success of 1945 Handicap champion Stymie who represented the first outstanding racehorse with close (3x3) inbreeding to Big Red. The following season, Jeffords duplicated the pattern by sending Ace Card, one of his best granddaughters of Man o' War to Red's grandson Firethorn and got the very useful brown colt Post Card who won eight stakes over four years in Maryland, Delaware and New Jersey.

Firethorn's best daughter and his lone source of perpetuity was the Whitney-bred Flyweight, a multiple stakes winner who became an important matron whose descendants include Grade 1 winners Editor's Note, Hennessy and Family Style.

As for Halcyon, he was just the right kind of mid-range outside stallion to have a shot at Faraway. A son of Broomstick whose third dam was a half-sister to Hastings, Halcyon figured to do particularly well with Man o' War broodmares. Even though he never became a particularly good sire, a second strain of Hasting's dam, Cinderella, appeared in a majority of the dams of Halcyon's better progeny including his best son Loyal Legion. Bred by Walter Jeffords, the gelding won a number of important contests including the Manhattan and Saratoga Handicaps.

The daughters of Red also did well with Blue Larkspur, standing at Col. E. R. Bradley's Idle Hour Farm only several miles from Faraway. Horse of the Year (1929) Blue Larkspur was out of a Sundridge-line mare and featured inbreeding to his fourth dam Padua in Formula One formation.

The best son of Blue Larkspur foaled at Faraway was Blue Swords, bred by Riddle and sold at the Saratoga yearlings sale for $3,300. He was another colt with the misfortune of being from the same crop as a standout Triple Crown winner. In this case, Blue Swords had to settle for bridesmaid status within his generation, running second to Count Fleet on several occasions including the 1943 Kentucky Derby and Preakness. When Blue Swords went to stud, his best daughter, Acorn Stakes winner Nothirdchance, was inbred 3x4 to Man o' War, her sire from a Riddle family, her dam from a Jeffords family. She went on to become the dam of influential sire Hail To Reason.

There were other more obscure outside stallions supported by Riddle and Jeffords that also proved to be well chosen. One of these, Trace Call, was an American-bred son of the unfashionable English sire Call Boy who enjoyed but one victory from 15 starts at the track. Trace Call's pedigree did show a rare strain from Peter, the sire of his third dam, who was a full brother to Pauline, the third dam of Fair Play (see Figure 1). His pedigree also demonstrated inbreeding to Rock Sand's granddam St. Marguerite. After a few good runners from his early crops, Samuel Riddle sent a couple of his Man o' War mares to Trace Call over several seasons and was rewarded with the stallion's two richest offspring, the filly Rampart and the colt War Trophy, both foals of 1942.

Rampart was a quite formidable race mare. Riddle sold her privately as a two-year-old to Mrs. H. K. Haggerty. Best at age six when winning six stakes, she became the first of only two distaffers to win the Gulfstream Park Handicap, shocking Horse of the Year Armed. She is still remembered at that track with the Grade 2 Rampart Handicap. She is also the matriarch of a very successful family whose descendants include California champion Belle's Flag.

War Trophy won the Bushwick Hurdle Handicap as a three-year-old for Glen Riddle Farms. Later on, he was sold privately to the Mimosa Farm, for which he annexed the Rhode Island Handicap and the Riggs Handicap when beating the Jeffords' Loyal Legion.

Another unconventional outside stallion used by the Faraway team was *Easton, a French-bred multiple stakes winner in England where he placed in several classic events. After five disappointing crops in Europe, he was imported to New Jersey where he fit very nicely into the plans of Jeffords with a broodmare prospect fresh off the track.

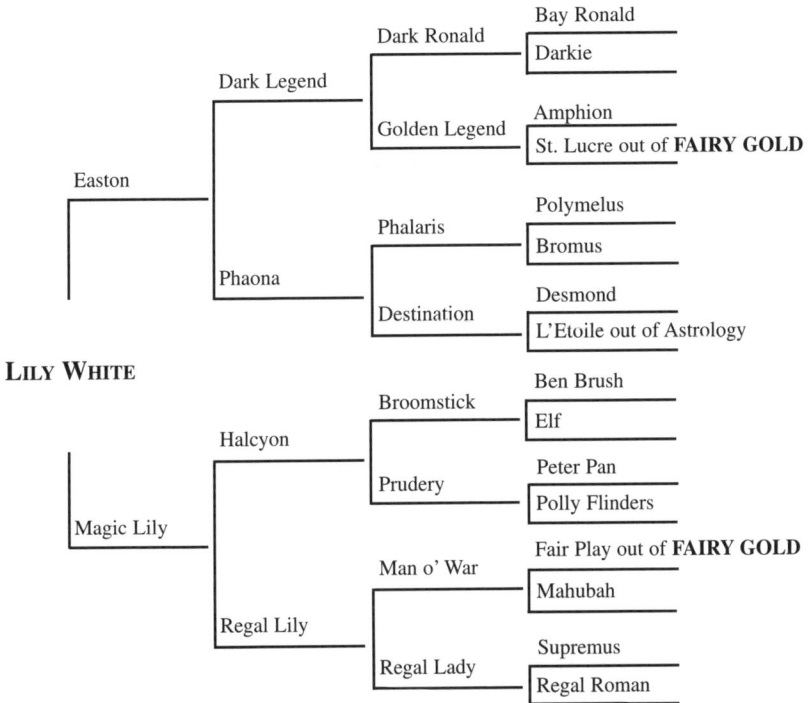

LILY WHITE

			Bay Ronald
		Dark Ronald	Darkie
	Dark Legend		Amphion
		Golden Legend	St. Lucre out of **FAIRY GOLD**
Easton			Polymelus
		Phalaris	Bromus
	Phaona		Desmond
		Destination	L'Etoile out of Astrology
			Ben Brush
		Broomstick	Elf
	Halcyon		Peter Pan
		Prudery	Polly Flinders
Magic Lily			Fair Play out of **FAIRY GOLD**
		Man o' War	Mahubah
	Regal Lily		Supremus
		Regal Lady	Regal Roman

The key to this mating was the third dam of Easton's sire, Dark Legend: the great Belmont mare Fairy Gold. For good measure, as illustrated in Figure 1, Easton's fourth dam was Star Shoot's dam, Astrology, also from the family of Fair Play.

The resultant filly Lily White won for the Jeffords, in 1952, their third Alabama Stakes in four years, their fourth victory in the race going back to Lily White's granddam Regal Lily 15 years earlier.

Another interesting pedigree that illustrates the unabashed practice of female family inbreeding at Faraway is that of Commonwealth whose dam was a half sister to the Jeffords-bred Travers winner Mars.

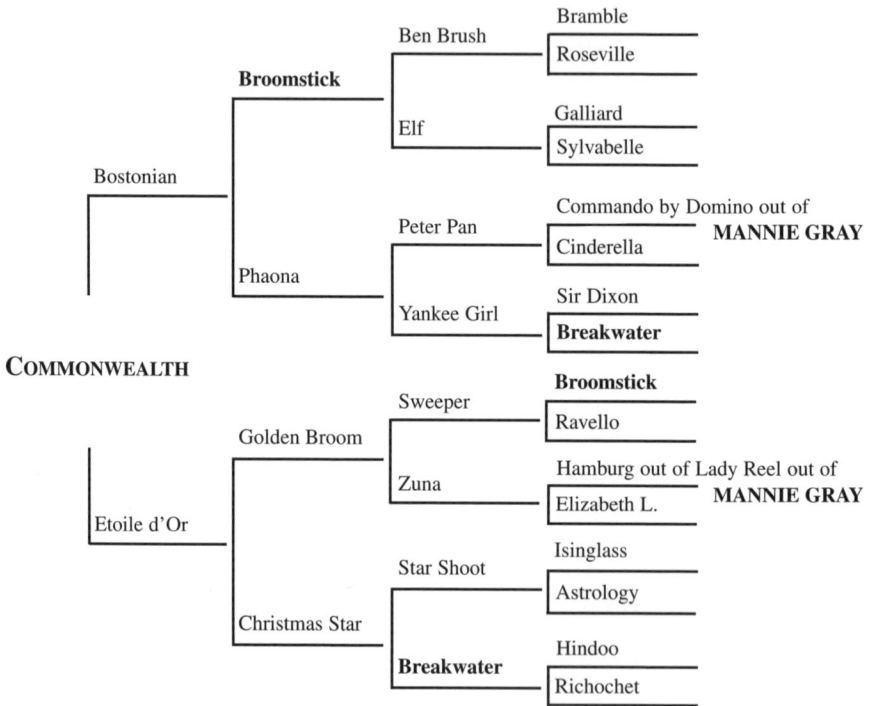

```
                                                              Bramble
                                           Ben Brush
                                                              Roseville
                             Broomstick
                                                              Galliard
                                           Elf
                                                              Sylvabelle
              Bostonian
                                                              Commando by Domino out of
                                           Peter Pan                              MANNIE GRAY
                                                              Cinderella
                             Phaona
                                                              Sir Dixon
                                           Yankee Girl
                                                              Breakwater
COMMONWEALTH
                                                              Broomstick
                                           Sweeper
                                                              Ravello
                             Golden Broom
                                                              Hamburg out of Lady Reel out of
                                           Zuna                                   MANNIE GRAY
                                                              Elizabeth L.
              Etoile d'Or
                                                              Isinglass
                                           Star Shoot
                                                              Astrology
                             Christmas Star
                                                              Hindoo
                                           Breakwater
                                                              Richochet
```

Commonwealth's third dam, the Hindoo mare Breakwater, was also the third dam of his sire, the Harry Payne Whitney-bred Preakness winner Bostonian, creating Formula One inbreeding to their accomplished tribe. His pedigree also includes inbreeding to the families of Domino and Hamburg. In his best race, Commonwealth beat his more talented stablemate Firethorn in a 1934 juvenile stakes at Bowie. The following season he ran 10th for the Jeffords in the Kentucky Derby.

A DAY IN THE LIFE OF MAN O' WAR

Man o' War was 20 years old last March. That is old age for a horse, but his life is little changed from what it was when he first went to the stud. His weight has increased from 1,000 pounds to around 1,375, and the fine racing lines have given way to a slightly potbellied appearance, but he is still strong and vigorous, and still likes to run. He lives in a box stall 20 feet square, which is always covered a foot deep with straw. Three similar box stalls fill up the rest of the stud stable; two of them are occupied by Big Red's sons, Crusader and American Flag, and the third now stands vacant, waiting for the time when War Admiral will retire to the stud. Other horses have come and gone. Among them was Golden Broom, Big Red's early rival, but Golden Broom wilted and lost this race to Man o' War, as he had lost the other; he died in 1935. Man o' War shows no signs of senility. From the first of October until the close of the breeding season, late in June, he is under saddle. Just as in his racing days, he is worked up to the peak of condition by a gradual increase in exercise – first walking and jogging, then getting up to galloping six to eight miles a day. And at the end of the season he is "unwound," just as he used to be, by a tapering off of exercise. He has a private two-acre paddock in which to ramble as he pleases – all day if the sun is not too hot, otherwise at night. Out there, he plays with the farm dogs, challenging them to come in, then chasing them out. He eats three times a day – at five o'clock, 11, and four. At each meal he gets three quarts of heavy rolled oats. His hay, a mixture of red clover and timothy, is shipped from Michigan; his green food is the Kentucky blue grass in his paddock. He is just about the biggest stallion in the blue-grass country, and he would eat even more if he could get it; he has never lost his appetite. His retinue now consists of his colored groom, Will Harbut; Will's son Robert, who rides him; a stableman, and a night watchman. Insured for $500,000, he is under the eye of one of these men every minute. Most of the time during the day Harbut or one of the others is in the barn or standing outside. They have a room in an adjoining building, in which they can go when it is cold; it has extra large windows which command a view of the side door of the barn, and the front door at such times is locked on the inside. If visitors appear, a man is quickly at their side, ready to show them around, but watchful. At four o'clock visiting hours are over, and at five the night watchman comes on duty, and stays until the others return at five in the morning.

Nearing 80 now, Riddle has recently built a small house just a few steps from Man o' War's barn, where he and Mrs. Riddle can go for a few days or weeks occasionally to be near the founder of their racing fortunes. It pleases Riddle that people still drive out to see the horse just as much as they did when he first retired – three thousand a month come, on the average, except in the winter.

Arthur Bartlett, *The New Yorker*,
December 18th, 1937

One of the men alleged to have offered astronomical figures to possess Big Red was movie mogul Louis B. Mayer who was said to have offered up $1 million in 1939 for the 22-year-old stallion. In Mary (Fleming) Simon's fine book, *A History of the Thoroughbred in California*, Riddle is quoted to have responded, "Tell Mr. Mayer that Man o' War is not for sale at any price. I don't know what he wants with him, but I think he might want to use him in the pictures and I wouldn't want that. He wouldn't know how to treat the old fellow. He is happy and contented where he is, and everyone knows just what to do for him; and that's the way I want it."

Mayer bided his time before haltering one of Red's good grandsons at the 1940 Saratoga yearling sale. A Blenheim II colt bred at Faraway from the Man o' War mare Gas Bag, the colt sold for just $3,500, owing to a curb. Given the name Thumbs Up, he went on to win the coveted 1945 Santa Anita Handicap and earnings of $249,290 for his proud owner.

Mayer was also responsible for sending to Man o' War's court, in 1940, the best producing mare he was ever bred to. This was the unraced La France, by Sir Gallahad III, already the dam of 1937 juvenile filly champion Jacola and 1939 Derby and Belmont winner Johnstown. The resultant chestnut colt, Free France, was a mediocre runner ($5,285; two wins) and even worse as a California stallion (0 SWs), again, only proving that 'not every kernel of corn will pop.'

FARAWAY STALLIONS IN THE POST-MAN O' WAR ERA

War Admiral's reign as premier sire at Faraway Farm marked the second half of the Riddle/Jeffords era.

By the time "The Admiral" joined his legendary sire in the stallion barn at Faraway Farm for the 1940 season, Big Red was already in the sunset of his great career at stud. His initial public fee was set at $1,500.

In 1945, like Man o' War before him, War Admiral became America's leading sire ($591,352, a single-year record) when his first crop was only four years of age. The Admiral's rapid ascent in the stallion ranks made dealing with the retirement of "the big horse" a lot easier for the franchise. The baton was passed, reluctantly and yet necessarily, but to a most worthy scion.

War Admiral's early success was largely due to the mares sent to him from Col. Edward R. Bradley's Idle Hour Stock Farm. Included were Baby League, who got Hall of Fame filly Busher, and Baba Kenny, the dam of Spinaway winner Bee Mac who also beat the boys in the 1943 Hopeful Stakes.

Mrs. Riddle greets War Admiral.

In 1945, obviously still enamored with Man o' War's blood, Louis B. Mayer paid Col. Bradley $50,000 for the War Admiral filly Busher at the beginning of her three-year-old season, having already been a champion at two. She responded for her new barn with a Horse of the Year campaign. Performing well beyond her peers, Busher took on and beat the best older male horses in training as well.

Never coming close to owning Man o' War, Mayer still had a lot of fun with Red's grandchildren.

Bradley's mares were previously unavailable to Big Red because of the Colonel's chronic aversion to the progeny of Fair Play and Man o' War. The self-described professional gambler, it seemed, had found he could not rely on members of this temperamental line to give their best performance when his money was down. On one occasion, Col. Bradley's famed advisor Olin Gentry was able to coax his boss into sending

Beaming Beauty, the dam of Derby winner Bubbling Over, to Man o' War despite the five grand-no return fee. When later informed that his mare had come up empty, the Colonel responded, "That's all right, Olin. I'd give $5,000 any time to keep Man o' War off the farm!"

Since, however, War Admiral was an atypical Man o' War in appearance, taking up much more like his dam's sire, the smallish brown Sweep, Gentry was able to convince Bradley to send some of his best mares to serve The Admiral as some of his first covers. The results were providential.

Busher's pedigree would serve as a template for a remarkable affinity that was to develop between her sire and granddam, the French-bred foundation matriarch *La Troienne (fam. #1-s). In all, War Admiral sired a total of 22 foals out of the daughters and granddaughters of La Troienne, eight (36 percent) of which became stakes winners.

Courtesy Keeneland Library

La Troienne

Interestingly, this cross revisited the advantages of duplicating strains from the Maid of Masham family since La Troienne's 4th dam was sired by the very obscure sire Timothy who was a full brother to Pauline, the third dam of War Admiral's grandsire Fair Play (see Figure 1). Idle Hour later showed the union to be effective in reverse, as well, when they sent the young War Admiral mare Bee Mac to their champion Bimelech, by Blue Larkspur out of La Troienne, and got his best son Better Self ($383,925; Carter H., etc.).

After Bradley's death in 1946, success with War Admiral and La Troienne-line mares continued under Ogden Phipps, who acquired several of the Colonel's best broodmares. Busanda, the Phipps-bred daughter of War Admiral, became an outstanding handicap mare and later produced the great runner and sire Buckpasser.

As a final tribute to the Colonel, Riddle attempted his own variation on the reverse of the War Admiral/La Troienne cross when he bred War Admiral's full sister Our Colors to Bimelech and got the 1950 colt named Bradley, winner of several important juvenile events.

This series of interactions with the bloodstock of Col. Bradley was part of a trend in the stud career of War Admiral. In general, the outside breeders who did best with him (see Table 8) were the ones with farms concurrently standing prominent stallions who were being success-fully supported by the broodmares of Riddle and Jeffords. The blending of Man o' War blood with these compatible outside lines in this way became beneficial for Riddle and Jeffords as well as their elite breeding partners. In all, a series of symbiotic relationships were taking place, including some that would help in shaping the evolving American breed.

Table 8 lists War Admiral's 40 stakes winners according to career earnings. It demonstrates that the same target ancestors complementary to the families in Man o' War's pedigree were also exceptionally common in the dams of War Admiral's best offspring.

Table 8 also shows that the mares War Admiral did best with often carried ancestors descending from the same key families as those appearing in the pedigree of War Admiral's dam, Brushup. Target ances-tors Swynford and Chaucer were full and half brothers, respectively, to Harry of Hereford, the sire of War Admiral's granddam, creating inbreed-ing to their dam, the great English matriarch Canterbury Pilgrim. Target ancestors Pennant and John P. Grier (Man o' War's toughest foe on the track) were from the same tribe as War Admiral's broodmare sire, Sweep, creating inbreeding to their common matron Belle Rose.

128

Table 8

War Admiral's Stakes Winners
(listed according to earnings)

Stakes Winner	Dam (Race Record)	Broodmare Sire [Breeder]	Earnings	Target Ancestor(s)	Racing Distinctions
BUSHER ch. f. 1942	Baby League (w) +	Bubbling Over [B]	$334,035	Snd / O / Hmb	1946 HOY, champion at 2 & 3
SEARCHING b. f. 1952	Big Hurry (SW) +	Black Toney [P]	$327,381	O	Gallorette H. (2X), Diana H. (2X)
ADMIRAL VEE ch. c. 1952	Yankee Flirt (w)	Blenheim II [R]	$315,795	Swn / FP-RS	Saratoga H., Paumonok H., etc.
KILMORAY br. g. 1959	Level Sands (SP)	Mahmoud [X]	$250,134	Swn / Hmb / RH	Toboggan H., New Year's Day H.
COLD COMMAND b. c. 1949	Monsoon (SW)	Mahmoud [W]	$206,225	Pnt / Swn	Saratoga H., Westchester H., etc.
BLUE PETER b. c. 1946	Carillon (w)	Case Ace [Ro]	$189,185	O / Snd / FP-RS / Pnt	Champion 2 YO colt, Futurity S.
BUSANDA blk. f. 1947	Businesslike (up) +	Blue Larkspur [P]	$182,460	Snd / O	Saratoga Cup (2X), Alabama S.
WAR COMMAND br. g. 1950	Canina (SW)	Bull Dog [X]	$158,440	O	Display Handicap
ADMIRAL DRAKE ch. c. 1947	Invoke (SW)	Teddy [Ro]	$145,325	JPG / O	American H., Argonaut H., etc.
WAR DATE br. f. 1942	Late Date (SW)	Hourless [X]	$139,755	- - -	Beldame H., Ladies H., etc.
NAVY PAGE ch. c. 1950	Our Page (SW)	Blue Larkspur [X]	$127,322	Snd / Hmb / SS	Jerome H., Toronto Cup H., etc.
BLUE BANNER b. f. 1952	Risque Blue (u)	Blue Larkspur [X]	$121,175	Snd / SS / O	Test H., Distaff H., Firenze H. etc.
WAR JEEP ch. c. 1942	Alyearn (up)	Blue Larkspur [Ro]	$108,235	Snd / Pldt	Remsen H., Jamaica H., etc.
TAVISTOCK ch. c. 1944	Tavy (w)	St. Germans [J]	$106,930	Swn / Hmb	Interborough H., 2nd Remsen H.
BRIC A BAC ch. c. 1941	Bloodroot (SP)	Blue Larkspur [B]	$103,225	Snd	San Juan Capistrano H., etc.
WAR KING blk. g. 1947	Guarded Queen (w)	On Watch [X]	$99,560	RH	Vosburgh Handicap
PARNASSUS b. c. 1950	Uvira II (SW)	Umidwar [X]	$92,125	Swn	Bourgainville Turf Handicap
WAR PIPER ch. c. 1951	Evening Tide (SW)	Bull Dog [C]	$89,675	O / FP-RS	Roseben H., 2nd Hopeful S., etc.
BEYLERBEY br. c. 1950	Bridal Flower (SW) +	Challenger II [X]	$89,194	Swn / O	Turf Paradise H., etc.
SAILED AWAY ch. c. 1949	Gentle Tryst (SP)	Sir Gallahad III [X]	$88,873	RH / O	Narragansett Special
ICARIAN ch. g. 1951	Legend Bearer (SP)	The Porter [W]	$84,854	FR / O	Aqueduct Handicap
MR BUSHER ch. c. 1946	Baby League (w) +	Bubbling Over [B]	$83,875	Snd / O / Hmb	Arlington Futurity, etc.

Stakes Winner	Dam (Race Record)	Broodmare Sire [Breeder]	Earnings	Target Ancestor(s)	Racing Distinctions
BROTHER TEX br. c. 1952	Our Page (SW)	Blue Larkspur [X]	$77,633	Snd / Hmb / SS	Breeders' Futurity S., Sanford S.
GREAT CAPTAIN blk/br. c. 1949	Big Hurry (SW) +	Black Toney [P]	$74,415	O	Saratoga Cup, San Marcos H.
NAVY CHIEF b. c. 1947	Sari Omar (w)	Sir Gallahad III [X]	$57,190	O / FP-RS	Great American S.
CABLE br. c. 1943	Miss Brief (w)	Sickle [X]	$56,880	Cha	Yankee S., 3rd Belmont S.
INHERITANCE b. f. 1945	Heritage (w)	Pharamond II [X]	$56,610	Cha / Snd	Matron Stakes
IRON MAIDEN b. f. 1941	Betty Derr (SW)	Sir Gallahad III [X]	$52,590	SS / O	Del Mar H., 2nd Vanity H., etc.
GRAND ADMIRAL ch. c. 1944	Grand Flame (w)	Grand Time [X]	$51,720	- - -	Saratoga Special, East View S.
WAR WATCH br. c. 1943	Watch Her (w)	On Watch [X]	$49,805	- - -	Absecon Handicap
VICE ADMIRAL ch. c. 1941	Mary Keen (w)	Victorian [X]	$45,805	Hmb	Jockey Club Handicap
FIRST REPEATER br. c. 1948	Blue Skimmer (w)	Johnstown [X]	$45,350	FP-RS / Snd	Christopher J. Fitzgerald H.
BEE MAC b. f. 1941	Baba Kenny (SW)	Black Servant [B]	$44,900	Snd	Hopeful S., Spinaway S.
WEE ADMIRAL ch. c. 1943	Little Nymph (SW)	Bull Dog [X]	$42,815	O	Bahamas H., 2nd Flamingo S.
THE ADMIRAL br. c. 1946	Big Hurry (SW) +	Black Toney [P]	$37,225	O	Tremont S., U.S. Hotel S.
BREAUX dkb/br. c. 1957	Boot All (SW)	All Boots [R]	$35,097	Cha / Hmb / O	Youthful S., 3rd Kentucky H.
MAKE A PLAY b. f. 1951	Spiral Pass (SW)	Pharamond II [C]	$33,650	Cha	Astarita S., Marguerite S.
BENBOW dkb/br. g. 1948	Invoke (SW)	Teddy [Ro]	$32,815	JPG / O	Tom Roby Steeplechase S., etc.
STRIKING b. f. 1947	Baby League (w) +	Bubbling Over [P]	$32,625	Snd / O / Hmb	Schuylerville S., 2nd Selima S.
WAR FAN br. f. 1944	Fantine (SP)	Whichone [X]	$26,275	Hmb	Pollyanna Stakes

Dams' Race Record:
u = unraced
up = unplaced
p = placed
w = winner
SP = stakes placed
SW = stakes winner

Breeder:
B = Col. E.R. Bradley
P = Ogden Phipps
R = Samuel D. Riddle
J = Walter M. Jeffords
W = C.V. Whitney
Ro = Joseph Roebling
C = Coldstream Stud
X = other

Target ancestors with Man o' War's pedigree
Snd = Sundridge   Hmb = Hamburg
SS = Star Shoot   RH = Roi Herode
FR = Friar Rock   O = Orme
Pldt = Plaudit

+ = descendants of La Troienne
FP-RS = Fair Play - Rock Sand cross

Target ancestors with Brushup's pedigree
Cha = Chaucer   Swn = Swynford
Pnt = Pennant   JPG = John P. Grier

Another characteristic inbreeding pattern in a number of War Admiral's stakes winners occurred when their dam carried the blood of a male or female ancestor who, like Man o' War, demonstrated the Fair Play-Rock Sand cross (see Table 2). This would be another pattern that reappeared over several generations in the pedigrees of important individuals.

The pedigree of Joseph M. Roebling's 1948 juvenile champion Blue Peter expresses several of these relationships. His dam, Carillon, carried the target ancestors Orme and Sundridge, complementary to Man o' War's pedigree as well as Pennant from Sweep's family and Mad Hatter, of the Fair Play-Rock Sand cross.

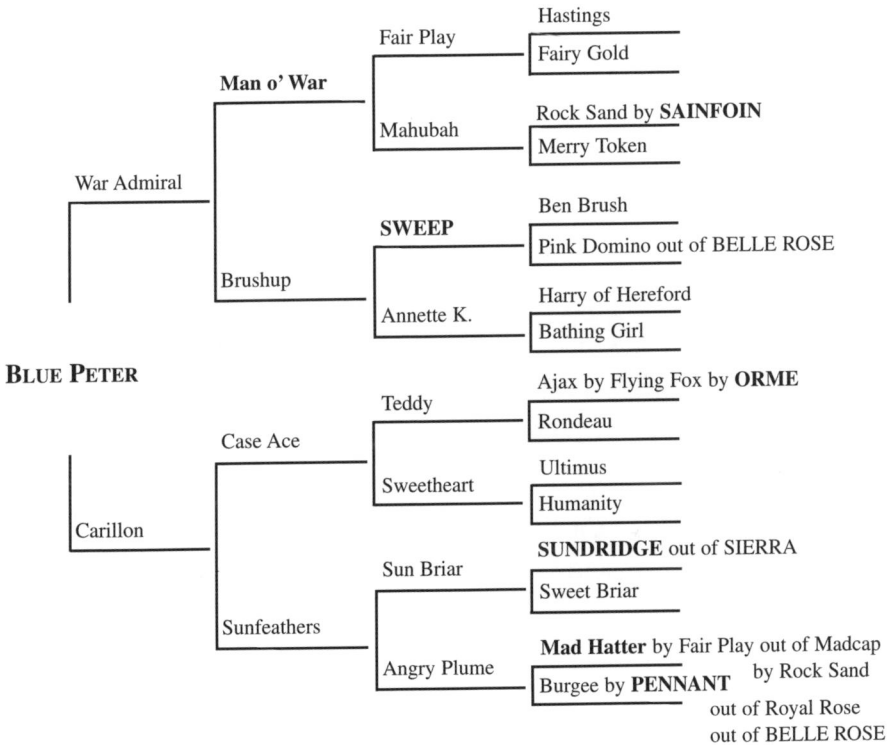

```
                                              Hastings
                               Fair Play
                                              Fairy Gold
                 Man o' War
                                              Rock Sand by SAINFOIN
                               Mahubah
                                              Merry Token
   War Admiral
                                              Ben Brush
                               SWEEP
                                              Pink Domino out of BELLE ROSE
                 Brushup
                                              Harry of Hereford
                               Annette K.
                                              Bathing Girl
BLUE PETER
                                              Ajax by Flying Fox by ORME
                               Teddy
                                              Rondeau
                 Case Ace
                                              Ultimus
                               Sweetheart
                                              Humanity
   Carillon
                                              SUNDRIDGE out of SIERRA
                               Sun Briar
                                              Sweet Briar
                 Sunfeathers
                                              Mad Hatter by Fair Play out of Madcap
                               Angry Plume                                    by Rock Sand
                                              Burgee by PENNANT
                                                            out of Royal Rose
                                                            out of BELLE ROSE
```

Since the Riddle and Jeffords broodmare bands were saturated with the blood of Man o' War by the late 1930s, the two found themselves limited in their opportunities to breed to War Admiral.

It would not be until 1952, a year after Samuel Riddle died, that his mare Yankee Flirt produced War Admiral's richest son, Admiral Vee. She was by the imported Blenheim II, a grandson of Swynford whose obscure full brother Harry of Hereford had sired War Admiral's granddam Annette K. By that time, inbreeding to their common dam, Canterbury Pilgrim, was becoming a recurring pattern in the pedigrees of important individuals on both sides of the Atlantic. Out of a Mad Hatter mare, Yankee Flirt's cross with War Admiral also duplicated the Fair Play-Rock Sand cross.

War Admiral [371 foals; 40 SWs (11 percent)] appeared in the top 20 on the annual U.S. sires rankings a total of 12 times. He was also credited with broodmare sire championships in 1962 and 1964. A truly great sire of distaff runners and broodmares, War Admiral never had a son that effectively carried on Man o' War's male line. That would be left to his stablemate War Relic.

War Relic

On the racetrack, War Relic was probably the third best three-year-old colt of his generation. In 1943, he became the last son of Man o' War to return to Faraway for the purpose of carrying on his newly retired sire's legacy.

A particularly unruly sort, War Relic [297 foals; 14 SWs (five percent)] would never prove to be a particularly consistent stallion. His record of five percent stakes winners was about the same as the other Man o' War stallions at Faraway who were deemed to be relative disappointments (Crusader, Mars and Boatswain).

The big difference in War Relic's case was his ability to sire several very good runners, one, in particular, who was potent enough to carry on his male line into the 21st century. That son was Harry Isaac's Intent who won the Santa Anita Maturity (now the Strub Stakes) as well as two runnings of the San Juan Capistrano Handicap.

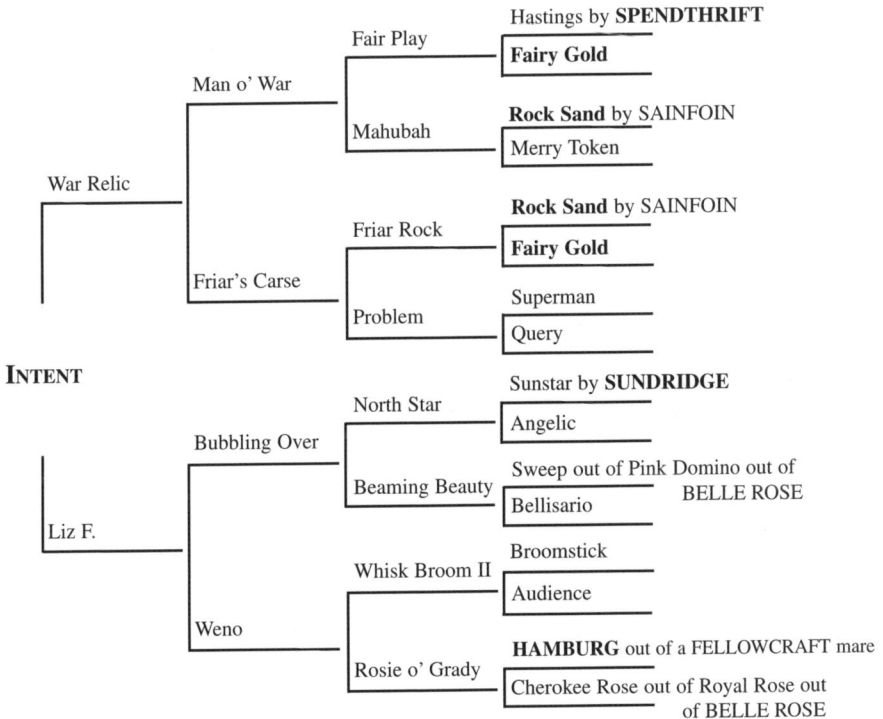

		Fair Play	Hastings by **SPENDTHRIFT**
	Man o' War		**Fairy Gold**
		Mahubah	**Rock Sand** by SAINFOIN
War Relic			Merry Token
		Friar Rock	**Rock Sand** by SAINFOIN
	Friar's Carse		**Fairy Gold**
		Problem	Superman
INTENT			Query
		North Star	Sunstar by **SUNDRIDGE**
	Bubbling Over		Angelic
		Beaming Beauty	Sweep out of Pink Domino out of BELLE ROSE
Liz F.			Bellisario
		Whisk Broom II	Broomstick
	Weno		Audience
		Rosie o' Grady	**HAMBURG** out of a FELLOWCRAFT mare
			Cherokee Rose out of Royal Rose out of BELLE ROSE

Intent's pedigree included a fascinating network of female family inbreeding patterns. His sire, War Relic, was himself closely inbred 3x3 to Fairy Gold as well as Rock Sand. His dam, Liz F., carried the cross of

Sweep and Pennant's full sister Cherokee Rose (Intent's fourth dam) creating inbreeding to their common granddam Belle Rose. Liz F. also carried the blood of Sundridge and Hamburg complementing the pairing between sire and dam.

War Relic appeared in the top 20 on the annual U.S. sires rankings three times (1950-52). His first exceptional son was the jet black colt Relic, winner of the 1947 Hopeful Stakes. War Relic became leading juvenile sire in 1950 when his son Battlefield was named two-year-old colt champion.

Remarkably, Battlefield was out of a daughter of Display (by Fair Play) and, thus, inbred 3x3 to Fair Play, further intensifying the inbreeding to his dam, Fairy Gold, 4x4x4. This caused Joe H. Palmer to conclude in *American Race Horses of 1950* that Battlefield's "pedigree was, apparently, deliberately calculated to frighten children."

In the summer of 1949, 88-year-old Riddle asked his old friend, Colonel P.T. Chinn, an outstanding judge of horses, to be his guest at the Saratoga sales to help select several yearlings for the Glen Riddle racing stable. The Colonel inspected the lot and by the evening of the first night of the sale he had chosen a few.

"Well, Colonel," rasped Riddle, "have you found me another Man o' War?"

"No, Boss," replied the Colonel amiably, "but I found one hell of a racehorse which Chinn would own if he had the bankroll. You had better buy him."

"How's he bred?"

"He's by War Relic."

"Colonel, you know I own War Relic and War Admiral. I have too much Fair Play blood. I want to diversify. I'm not going to buy anything by War Relic!"

The colt, soon known as Battlefield, was purchased by George D. Widener for just $4,500 and became the bargain of the year. After his champion two-year-old season, when winning 11 of 13 starts, Battlefield won eight more stakes events from ages three through five including the 1951 Travers holding off the Jeffords' Yildiz.

Relic was bred by Col. Bradley from the family of Blue Larkspur and was eventually exported to France where he forged a successful line that lasted several generations.

War Relic also sired Iltis, the granddam of In Reality, who became torch carrier of the Man o' War line with a pedigree featuring close inbreeding 3x3 to War Relic.

After War Relic's arrival at Faraway Farm, five more stallions would follow.

Teddy's Comet [232 foals; 12 SWs (five percent)] was relocated to Faraway from Texas in 1945. The Teddy stallion did a little better there with Man o' War mares including one from the Jeffords who produced his good son Sagittarius.

Jeffords' champion Pavot, by Case Ace, entered stud in 1948. Like Firethorn, he represented a maternal grandson of Man o' War returning to Faraway as a sire. Pavot [208 foals; 14 SWs (seven percent)] was a useful sort with at least a handful of producing daughters whose family descendants have kept his blood alive. Among these, the Jeffords-bred duo of Ampola and Pavonia, both closely inbred to Man o' War 3x3, would carve out particularly important clans.

Natchez, one of the Jeffords' four Travers winners, returned to Faraway in 1950. Son of Red's granddaughter Creole Maid, Natchez was sired by Jamestown whose dam, Mlle. Dazie, was by Fair Play and out of a Rock Sand mare, thus duplicating that auspicious cross. Natchez [42 foals; four SWs (10 percent)] died prematurely after only a couple of seasons, but did generate popular Santa Anita Handicap winner Bobby Brocato.

*Somali II [158 foals; six SWs (four percent)] was an English-bred stakes-placed son of Nasrullah that Riddle imported in 1950, only months before his own death. Riddle's estate would eventually breed his richest runner, War Council, out of a War Admiral mare, the same cross that had previously issued Nasrullah's English Derby-winning son Never Say Die.

The last stallion to arrive was Post Card, by Firethorn, in 1953. He would be the only Faraway stallion who was inbred to the farm's foundation sire. For whatever reasons, Post Card [23 foals; three SW (13 percent)] got hardly any outside mares. All three of his stakes winners were bred by the Jeffords.

The only two of Man o' War's top sons never to reach stud were the Jeffords' juvenile champion Scapa Flow and H.P. Gardner's Clyde Van Dusen.

Scapa Flow was a beautiful bay with a star and stripe on his face that developed bad ankles. He suffered a gruesome and fatal breakdown in the 1928 Brooklyn Handicap while contending, one furlong from home. Riddle always insisted Scapa Flow was the best colt Man o' War ever got.

Clyde Van Dusen was gelded after he was deemed "weedy" as a youngster. It was a decision made, ironically, by horseman Clyde Van Dusen who raised his namesake and trained him to win the 1929 Kentucky Derby.

MAN O' WAR STALLIONS AT OTHER FARMS

The controversies regarding the management of Man o' War's sire career warrants a review of Red's sons who served at stud at farms other than Faraway.

Table 9 compares the sire records of Red's sons at Faraway Farm with those standing at other farms. Heading up the list of outside stallions, Annapolis and Battleship were both outstanding sires of steeplechasers. Their influence is described in Chapter 8.

Table 9	MAN O' WAR's SONS at STUD		
	(who sired at least 1 American stakes winner)		
	Faraway Stallions		
	# Foals	Stakes Winners	SWs earning over $100,000
AMERICAN FLAG	183	16	1
BOATSWAIN*	123	6	0
CRUSADER*	120	6	0
MARS	87	4	0
WAR ADMIRAL	371	40	15
WAR RELIC	297	14	3

*many of Boatswain's and Crusader's foals were bred after they left Faraway Farm

MAN O' WAR's SONS at STUD

(who sired at least 1 American stakes winner)

Non-Faraway Stallions

	# Foals	Stakes Winners	SWs earning over $100,000
ANNAPOLIS +	77	12	3
BATTLESHIP +	58	11	2
BROADSIDE	82	3	0
BY HISSELF +	85	3	0
DRESS PARADE	127	1	0
FAIRY MANHURST	34	2	1
GENIE	58	2	0
HARD TACK	186	12	2
IDENTIFY	82	1	0
JEAN BART	119	2	0
KEARSARGE	40	1	0
MARINE	39	5	0
SAMMIE	30	3	0
SKY RAIDER	158	8	2
SON O' BATTLE	76	4	0
WAR GLORY	180	13	1
WAR HERO	110	1	0

+ = sire of steeplechase runners

Steeplechase racing aside, Table 9 confirms the point that no other farm enjoyed great success with Man o' War stallions.

The pedigrees of the few superior individuals sired by Red's sons standing at outside farms also usually demonstrated female family inbreeding patterns with their dams often carrying Man o' War's aforementioned target sires and families in their lineage. On other occasions, the inbreeding patterns involved families that appeared on the bottom half of Man o' War's sons' pedigrees.

Red's talented but bad-tempered son Genie [58 foals; two SWs (three percent)] went to W.S. Kilmer's Court Manor Stud in Virginia with a starting fee of $500. He died following a paddock accident after siring only four crops. Both of his stakes winners were fillies out of Sundridge-line mares.

Fairy Manhurst also went to Virginia where he sired only one very good filly, Gaffery (Selima and Santa Susana Stakes), whose pedigree demonstrated Formula One inbreeding to her third dam Fair Star, as well as duplication of the Fair Play-Rock Sand cross.

A. G. Vanderbilt's Identify was known at the track as a "rabbit" for his more famous stablemate Discovery. Upon retirement, Identify went to his owner's Sagamore Farm in Maryland where he also only sired one very good filly. Vanderbilt's 1941 juvenile filly champion Petrify's pedigree featured close inbreeding to Tracery and his full brother Trap Rock.

War Glory went to Oakmead Farm in California where he was a fair sire, also doing best when bred to mares who contributed family strains complementary with his own pedigree.

It is quite telling, if not also ironic, that the only truly exceptional paternal grandson of Man o' War sired by an outside stallion was Seabiscuit, conqueror of Glen Riddle's War Admiral. Seabiscuit was by Hard Tack, a particularly nasty individual with an erratic race record. He had difficulty finding a farm, let alone mares, before Charles S. Howard bought his legendary son and, soon thereafter, set the sporting world on its ear. After Seabiscuit's exploits, Hard Tack was welcomed at Claiborne Farm and was afforded many opportunities but never sired anything close to that one again. Hard Tack was from the family of Ben Brush's sire, Bramble, and most of his stakes winners, including Seabiscuit, were from mares carrying their blood.

Actually, in a novel sense, the outside Man o' War stallion with the most clout was Tsukitomo (out of Alzada, by Sir Martin) who was imported 'in utero' to Imperial Japan and foaled in 1933. Never raced, he became the only one of Red's sons to sire all of his progeny in a foreign country. He appeared among Japan's top 10 leading sires a total of 10 times from 1941 to 1954 and was the sire of three Derby winners including 1955 Japanese Horse of the Year, O Tokitsu. As a sire of dams, Tsukitomo led the country's broodmare sire list four times.

In the summer of 1944, Harrie B. Scott, who had maintained a farm of his own during the 14 years he managed Faraway, turned the Riddle portion of the farm over to Charles Gribbin. In December of 1945, Gribbin went back to the racetrack to train the Riddle horses, entrusting the farm and horses to long-term Riddle employee Patrick O'Neill.

Most of the breeding success enjoyed by Riddle and the Jeffords can be divided into 10 distinct family groups. Nine of these tribes originated with the purchase of a select broodmare whose descendants were enriched with the blood of Man o' War.

Figure 2

FRIAR'S CARSE   #1-o
(Friar Rock)

WAR RELIC	SPEED BOAT		WAR KILT	Anchors Ahead
(Man o' War)	(Man o' War)		(Man o' War)	(Man o' War)

Swing Time	The Sward	**LEVEL BEST**
(Royal Minstrel)	(Sickle)	(Equipoise)

Ellendale
(Bimelech)

WAR AGE
(War Relic)

Friar's Carse was the only one of the nine foundation matriarchs at Faraway with a successful racing career. Riddle purchased her from California breeder John H. Rosseter along with her dam, Problem, prior to the 1924 breeding season. There is some debate as to whether the chestnut filly was acquired 'in utero,' making Riddle the official breeder, or if she was foaled before the transaction took place, allowing Rosseter to maintain that honor. Different sources show both horsemen as having bred Friar's Carse, but the definitive source, the *American Stud Book*, has Riddle listed as her official breeder.

Sired by Fair Play's half-brother Friar Rock, and from a good family, the Man o' War camp viewed this filly as an appealing prospect for racing and breeding. Riddle named her Friar's Carse after his ancient family manor along the River Nith near the southwest border of England and Scotland. She won five of seven starts for him including three stakes at the age of two when she was considered the best juvenile filly of the 1925 season.

Figure 2 illustrates the family tree of Friar's Carse with sires in parentheses, stakes winners in capital letters and champions in bold type.

When bred to Big Red, Friar's Carse produced War Relic, his sire's torch carrier, and three valuable daughters who went on to forge their own successful branches.

Cleveland sportsman Crispin Oglebay acquired, via Glen Riddle, the unraced filly Anchors Ahead who produced for him 1944 Spinaway Stakes winner Level Price, by Sickle. The Man o' War mare would ultimately become the sixth dam of 1996 juvenile filly champion Storm Song. Oglebay, certainly lucky with this family, also signed the sales ticket on a daughter of Anchors Ahead's full sister Speed Boat who became 1940 juvenile filly champion Level Best. Oglebay also owned Holystone (ch. c., 1931, out of Brush Along by Sweep), described as Man o' War's "best looking son – a model of beauty and form." Not much on the racetrack, Holystone was for years the ranking horse in U.S. show rings, in the hunter class.

Bred by Riddle late in his life, the stakes-winning colt War Age had an unusual pedigree. He was a son of War Relic out of a grand-daughter of his sire's full sister Speed Boat creating 1x3 inbreeding to the two siblings. Three decades later, horseman Robert E. Hibbert fashioned a variation on this theme when he bred 1982 juvenile champion colt Roving Boy. By Olden Times, a paternal grandson of War Relic, Roving Boy's dam was a granddaughter of War Relic's full sister War Kilt, forming the 3x3 family tandem.

War Age's full sister Ellen's Best would later become the dam of Belmont and Travers Stakes winner Hail To All, by Hail To Reason.

Another important family branch involved Speed Boat's oldest daughter, Swing Time, who Riddle sold as a yearling in 1936 to Brookmeade Farm for $6,200. A non-winner from eight starts, she never-theless became the granddam of that farm's best horse, Sword Dancer – America's 1959 Horse of the Year and sire of the great Damascus.

Walter Jeffords acquired Fleur (1932) from the paddocks of C.V. Whitney. Her pedigree featured the classic Whitney cross of Pennant with Broomstick mares. Fleur's dam, Forsythia, was a three-quarters sister to multiple stakes winner Whiskaway. Before the Whitney influence, most of Fleur's family was developed by Major Foxhall Daingerfield at Castleton Stud.

Figure 3

Fleur   #10-a
(Pennant)

```
                    Fleur          #10-a
                  (Pennant)
         ┌────────────┴────────────┐
     Coquelicot                 My Rose
     (Man o' War)                (Snark)
  ┌──────┼──────┐          ┌───────┴───────┐
PAVOT  Azalea  LOVAT     MOMUS        PORTSMOUTH
(Case Ace) (Sun Teddy) (Jamestown) (Natchez)  (Blue Prince)
         ↓
```

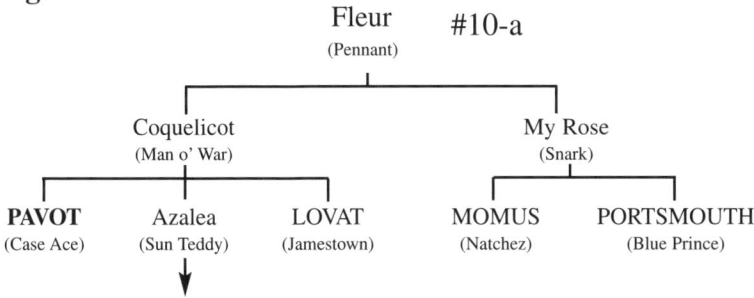

Fleur's most important immediate descendant, Pavot, was the product of the Case Ace-Man o' War cross. Shades of his uncle and Man o' War, a quarter of a century earlier, Jeffords stunned the racing world in late 1944 when he announced his undefeated juvenile champion would not be going to the Kentucky Derby the following spring.

"It is too early in the year to ask a three-year-old to go a mile and a quarter," Jeffords told *The Thoroughbred Record's* Neville Dunn. "I shant even nominate Pavot to the Derby because it is the only way I can keep my friends from betting on him in the winter books." When the colt did come back, he won the Belmont Stakes by five lengths. At four, Pavot took the rich Massachusetts Handicap over Gallorette and the Jockey Club Gold Cup, easily beating Stymie.

Pavot's half-sister Azalea is responsible for carrying on the tail-female line. She is the third dam of leading sire Riverman and the fifth dam of 2002 European Horse of the Year Rock Of Gibraltar.

Interestingly, on one of the few times Riverman was bred to a mare carrying Pavot blood, he sired European Group 1 champion Lahib, creating a very rare inbreeding pattern to Coquelicot (whose name in French is synonymous with Pavot, both meaning "poppy").

Bathing Girl was selected by William Allison for the Jeffords account at the 1920 December Tattersalls Sale at Newmarket for 800 British guineas ($3,075). Shortly after her arrival at Hinata Farm, she had a filly by Harry of Hereford, Annette K., named after famous Australian swimmer Annette Kellerman. Jeffords presented the young bay filly to his partner and uncle-by-marriage as a gift. Riddle subsequently bred

Annette K. to Sweep and got the diminutive bay filly Brushup (14.3 3/4 hands), dam of the best horse he ever bred, War Admiral.

Four years before the Admiral's Triple Crown season, his three-quarters brother War Glory was one of the best sophomores of 1933 winning five important stakes but showing an Achilles' heel when the track came up wet.

When Jeffords, a former naval officer, bred Bathing Girl to Man o' War he got the filly Seaplane, a term originally coined by Sir Winston Churchill to replace 'hydro-aeroplane' after the British leader experienced his first flight.

Figure 4

Bathing Girl   #11-g
(Spearmint)

Annette K.	TRITON	Seaplane
(Harry of Hereford)	(Golden Broom)	(Man o' War)

WAR GLORY   Brushup   Dinner Time
(Man o' War)   (Sweep)   (High Time)

Military Brush **WAR ADMIRAL** Our Colors   EIGHT THIRTY
(Man o' War)   (Man o' War)   (Man o' War)   (Pilate)

My Brush   BRADLEY
(Menow)   (Bimelech)

BRUSH BURN
(Bemborough)

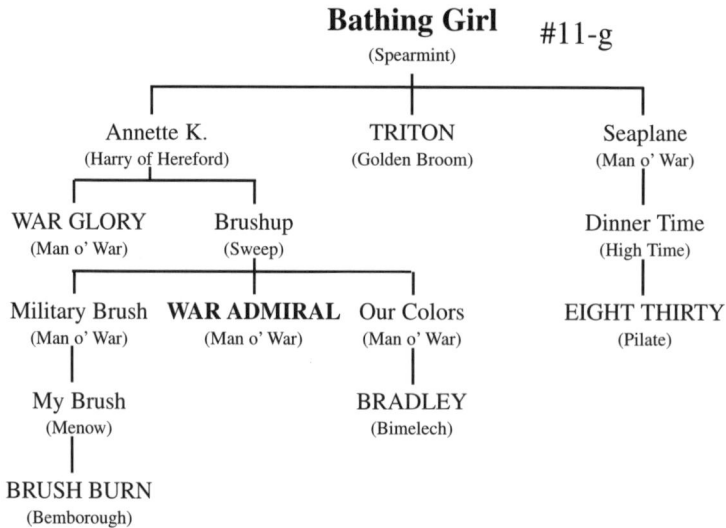

Two generations later, Seaplane became the granddam of George D. Widener's remarkable chestnut colt Eight Thirty (Racing Hall of Fame, Travers Stakes, Toboggan Handicap – twice, influential sire). Eight Thirty was by Pilate, a son of Friar Rock. His pedigree, then, featured the reverse of the Man o' War-Friar Rock cross that produced War Relic.

Bel Agnes was purchased by Jeffords from William Woodward's Belair Stud for $3,700 at the 1922 Saratoga yearling sale. Woodward consigned her to auction after she cut one of her legs in the field. Later, he commented that she was the only mare he ever regretted selling.

Bel Agnes was sufficiently regarded by the Jeffords camp to make her first two starts in juvenile stakes, but she finished last both times and never raced again. After her younger full brother Peanuts became a top handicap performer from 1925 to 1927 and her daughter Good As Gold became a multiple stakes winner, Bel Agnes was added to the book of Man o' War. She delivered Judy o' Grady, a very talented filly who never won a big race but ran second in several including Nellie Flag's Matron and Selima Stakes at two, as well as the Manhattan Handicap and Jockey Club Gold Cup (to stablemate Firethorn) at three.

Figure 5

Bel Agnes
(Ambassador IV)   #16-c

| GOOD AS GOLD | Judy o' Grady |
| (Golden Broom) | (Man o' War) |

| Irish Nora | WESTMINSTER | SNOW GOOSE |
| (Pharamond II) | (Bull Dog) | (Mahmoud) |

KISS ME KATE   Mrs. Arris   MERGANSER   Locust Time
(Count Fleet)   (Pavot)   (Pavot)   (Spy Song)

LEWISTON   FARAWAY SON
(Rasper II)   (Ambiopoise)

Blue Denim
(Blue Larkspur)

| GREEN BAIZE | SULEIMAN | TAHITI | Ampola | BLUE PRINCE | POLICEMAN DAY | Coque Blue | PIANO JIM |
| (Case Ace) | (Mahmoud) | (Polynesian) | (Pavot) | (Princequillo) | (Challedon) | (Daumier) | (Bemborough) |

MOONREINDEER
(Dark Star)

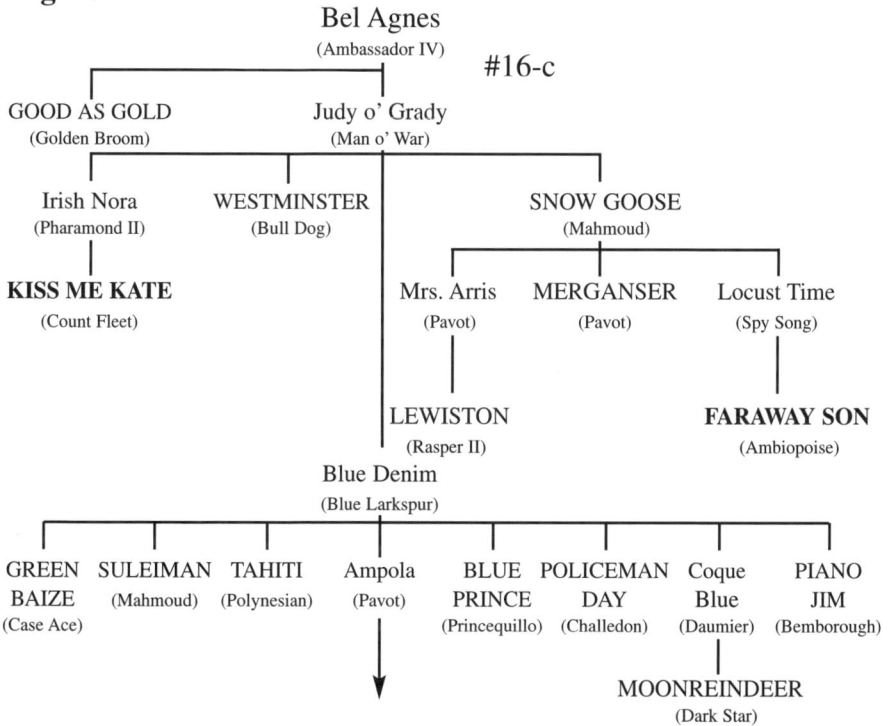

As illustrated in Figure 5, Judy o' Grady was a potent matriarch. Her daughter Blue Denim produced a half-dozen stakes winners for the Jeffords including their fourth Travers Stakes winner, Piano Jim. His half-brother Blue Prince had earlier been shipped to England where he won several important fixtures over three seasons. He was sixth of 22 in Never Say Die's Derby of 1954. The following season, Blue Prince ran second in the Ascot Gold Cup, that country's premiere stamina event for older horses.

Another interesting member of this family is the aptly named colt Faraway Son who was bred by Walter "Jeff" Jeffords Jr. after his father's death. Faraway Son was moved to France where he became a multiple Group 1 winning champion miler. At stud, his one claim to fame was 1979 American champion distaffer Waya whose dam was, quite remarkably, a daughter of Blue Prince, and, hence, inbred 4x4 to the tribe's true anchor, Judy o' Grady.

Blue Denim's daughter Ampola, sired by Pavot and closely inbred to Man o' War, is responsible for much of the subsequent success of this family. A modest winner, she was sold privately by Jeffords after her last start in early 1953. Ampola's descendants have come to comprise the tribe's most important contemporary branch. She is the second and third dam of influential sires Grey Dawn II and Green Dancer, respectively.

Figure 6

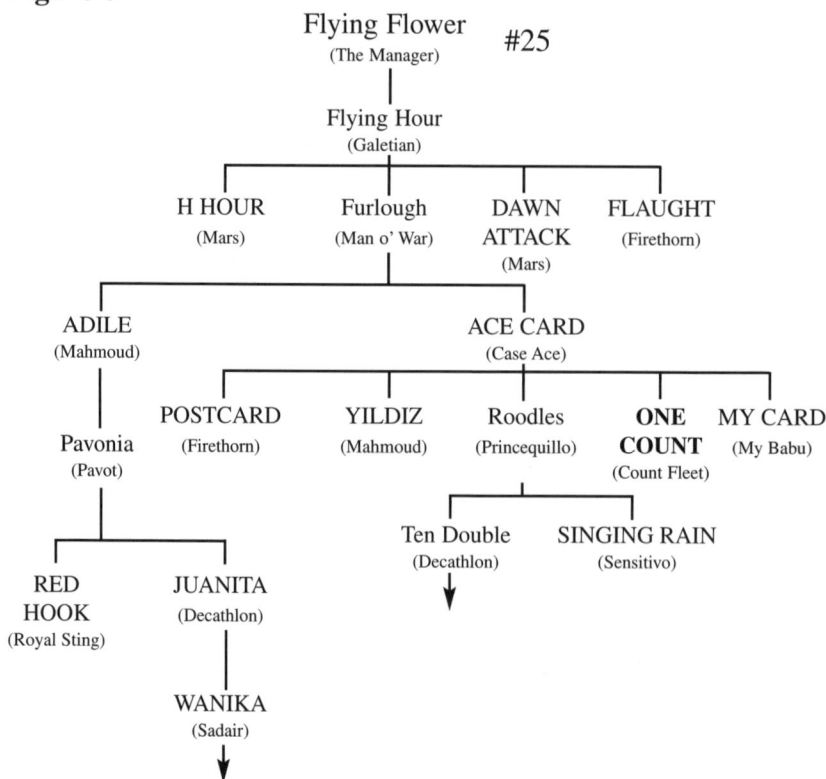

Flying Flower (1917), perhaps the least distinguished member of the early Jeffords broodmare band, initiated a family that "took off" when supplied with Man o' War's blood. By the undistinguished stallion The Manager and from a weak American family, it would seem her only appeal was that her sire was from the same family as the Jeffords' favorite colt, Golden Broom. Flying Flower was never bred to Big Red and her foals by Golden Broom and the other non-Man o' War-line stallions proved useless.

A generation later, however, one of her daughters, Flying Hour, produced three stakes winners when bred to Red's son Mars and grandson Firethorn. When given an opportunity with Man o' War, Flying Hour produced the invaluable broodmare Furlough, the true family anchor.

Furlough's daughter Ace Card, 1952 Broodmare of the Year, produced four stakes winners including One Count, co-Horse of the Year at age three. Her branch has flourished through her granddaughter Ten Double, the granddam of English three-year-old filly champion Mrs. Penny and the third dam of Hatoof, European filly champion and a champion turf mare in the U.S. as well.

Adile's best producing daughter Pavonia was closely inbred to Man o' War. This branch lives on today through Grade 3 winner Wanika, who was bred by Walter Jeffords Jr. carrying on the family tradition after both his parents had died. With time, Wanika became the third dam of 1994 juvenile filly champion Flanders who, in turn, produced 2000 three-year-old filly champion Surfside.

The most closely inbred Thoroughbred ever bred by Jeffords was a 1957 bay colt named Bavard whose sire, Pavot, and dam, Ace Card, were both by Case Ace and out of Man o' War mares! An interesting experiment, especially for such a valuable broodmare, but Bavard's only asset at the races was his durability ($15,386, 111 starts, three wins).

The unraced four-year-old filly Batanoea, in foal to Hainault, was selected by William Allison at the 1920 Tattersalls December sale and then imported by Walter Jeffords. The filly she foaled the next spring at Hinata Farm, Baton, was the daughter to carry on her female line.

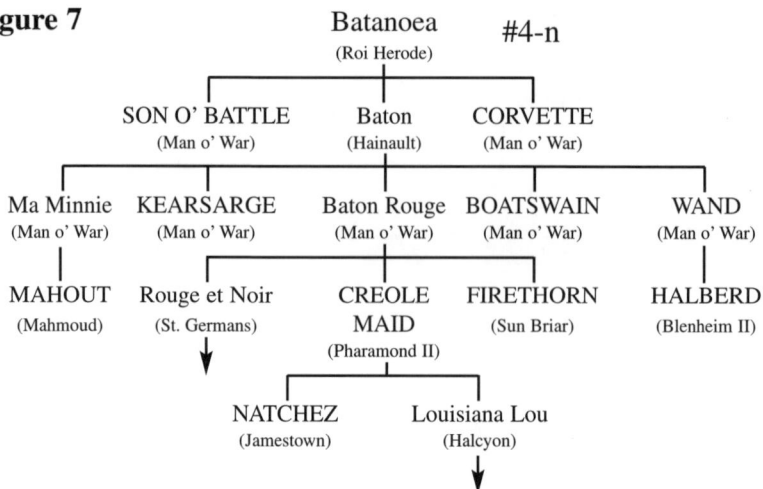

Figure 7

Batanoea
(Roi Herode)

#4-n

SON O' BATTLE
(Man o' War)

Baton
(Hainault)

CORVETTE
(Man o' War)

Ma Minnie
(Man o' War)

KEARSARGE
(Man o' War)

Baton Rouge
(Man o' War)

BOATSWAIN
(Man o' War)

WAND
(Man o' War)

MAHOUT
(Mahmoud)

Rouge et Noir
(St. Germans)

CREOLE
MAID
(Pharamond II)

FIRETHORN
(Sun Briar)

HALBERD
(Blenheim II)

NATCHEZ
(Jamestown)

Louisiana Lou
(Halcyon)

At Faraway Farm, Baton was bred exclusively to Man o' War and she responded by producing three stakes winners and two more stakes producers. Her son Boatswain was of top class, but very unlucky. He lost the 1932 Preakness by two heads and a poor ride. He then went wire-to-wire over a top field in the Withers, but subsequently arrived in Chicago for the American Derby injured while in transit, never to race again.

Boatswain's sister Baton Rouge produced Firethorn, Creole Maid and Rouge Et Noir, the latter becoming the second dam of Nothirdchance (Acorn S., etc.), dam of leading sire Hail To Reason. The descendants of Creole Maid's daughter Louisiana Lou include her grandson Admiral's Voyage (Wood Mem. S., etc.), who became the broodmare sire of leading sire Danzig.

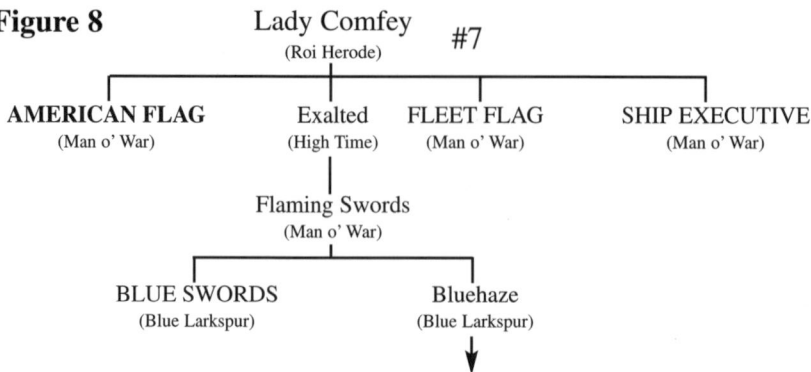

Figure 8

Lady Comfey
(Roi Herode)

#7

AMERICAN FLAG
(Man o' War)

Exalted
(High Time)

FLEET FLAG
(Man o' War)

SHIP EXECUTIVE
(Man o' War)

Flaming Swords
(Man o' War)

BLUE SWORDS
(Blue Larkspur)

Bluehaze
(Blue Larkspur)

The seven-year-old brown Roi Herode mare Lady Comfey was purchased in 1920 by William Allison at Newmarket for the account of Riddle. From Man o' War's first crop, she produced his first champion son, American Flag.

Argosie, a younger full sister to American Flag, was described by veteran George Conway as the best filly he ever trained, even though she never won a stakes race. She placed in several important events including a second to Racing Hall of Famer Top Flight in the 1932 Coaching Club American Oaks. For whatever reason, she had very little impact as a broodmare.

American Flag's three-quarter sister Flaming Swords produced Count Fleet's foil, Blue Swords, a talented but unlucky colt. She was later sold by Riddle to his farm manager, Harrie B. Scott, the breeder of Blue Swords' full sister Bluehaze whose daughter Dinner Partner created a very productive family branch for Buffalo Bills owner Ralph Wilson. The clan ultimately issued 1991 juvenile champion Arazi.

Figure 9

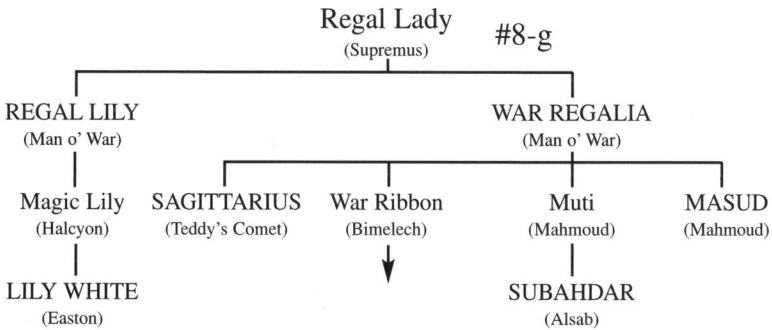

Regal Lady
(Supremus)   #8-g

REGAL LILY   WAR REGALIA
(Man o' War)   (Man o' War)

Magic Lily   SAGITTARIUS   War Ribbon   Muti   MASUD
(Halcyon)   (Teddy's Comet) (Bimelech)   (Mahmoud)   (Mahmoud)

LILY WHITE   SUBAHDAR
(Easton)   (Alsab)

Regal Lady (1928) was originally bred and owned by Hal Price Headley who imported her dam, Regal Roman by Roi Herode, from England in 1923. She was purchased by Jeffords as a yearling in the summer of 1929 and while she was herself only a modest winner, her older full sister Alcibiades was soon shown to be the best filly of her generation both at two and again at age three in 1930. With her Roi Herode blood and newly-decorated family connections, Jeffords saw Regal Lady as a worthy breeding partner with Man o' War.

Regal Lady's daughter Regal Lily won for the Jeffords their first Alabama Stakes in 1937. Three years later, the Alabama was taken by H.P. Headley's Man o' War filly Salaminia, a daughter of Alcibiades – in other words, Regal Lily's genetic full sister. Two generations later, Regal Lily's granddaughter Lily White captured the Jeffords' fourth Alabama.

Most of Regal Lady's best descendants since the end of the Faraway Farm dynasty have come via her granddaughter War Ribbon including 1985 Breeders' Cup Classic winner Proud Truth.

Figure 10

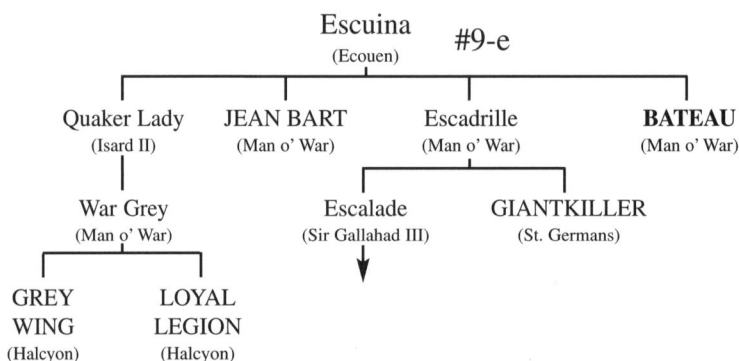

```
                    Escuina      #9-e
                    (Ecouen)
   ┌──────────┬────────────┬──────────────┬──────────┐
Quaker Lady   JEAN BART    Escadrille      BATEAU
(Isard II)    (Man o' War) (Man o' War)    (Man o' War)
   │                        ┌───────────┬───────┐
War Grey                    Escalade      GIANTKILLER
(Man o' War)                (Sir Gallahad III)  (St. Germans)
   ┌──────┬───────┐              ↓
GREY      LOYAL
WING      LEGION
(Halcyon) (Halcyon)
```

The French-bred four-year-old Escuina was imported in foal to Isard II in 1923. The best of her foals was Man o' War's best daughter Bateau. A co-champion filly and winner of the Coaching Club American Oaks at three, the rugged and powerful Jeffords charge came back at four to beat some of the best male handicappers in training on three occasions.

Despite all of the intervention by specialists, Bateau was a bitter disappointment at stud, proving completely barren. Of the 22 of Man o' War's 199 daughters that never produced a foal, Bateau easily represented the greatest opportunity unrealized.

Consequently, Bateau's unraced full sister Escadrille has provided the strongest branch of their dam through her daughter Escalade, subsequent fifth dam of three-year-old champion Snow Chief.

Riddle and Jeffords also did particularly well with a 10th key tribe, Family #4-m, the family of Whisk Broom II, H.P. Whitney's Racing Hall of Famer and successful sire.

Broodmares all descending from Whisk Broom's 3rd dam Red and Blue appear to have been a preference for Riddle and Jeffords. She was the fifth dam of champions Crusader and Scapa Flow, the sixth dam of Alabama Stakes heroine War Hazard as well as the eighth dam of War Admiral's richest son, Admiral Vee.

Five of these 10 tribes descended from so-called non-preferred maternal lines according to Bruce Lowe's "Figure System." Clearly, the Lowe dogma was never part of the Faraway game plan.

What all of these families did demonstrate was a dramatic and positive shift in the relative quality of their descendants once Man o' War's blood was introduced.

CHAPTER EIGHT

The Legacy of Man o' War
and Faraway Farm

"As I walked from the palatial stud barn at
Faraway Farm, I wondered to myself if I ever before had
seen, or ever would again see, under the same roof, a father
and son who have contributed so much to Turf history."

John H. Clark
The Thoroughbred Record,
December 21, 1946

A testament to Man o' War's greatness goes well beyond all the track records he smashed. It encompasses all the ways he came to be treated more like a human celebrity, by more people, than any other horse, before or since.

Red just took it all in. Faraway's veteran manager Harrie B. Scott called him the smartest horse he ever encountered.

While all horses share the universal birthday of January 1, Big Red's actual foaling date, March 29, was observed as a special occasion. He received telegrams, carrots and other tokens of recognition from all over the country. When Red turned 21 in 1938, his party in the stallion barn was broadcast coast-to-coast by famed race caller Clem McCarthy. Guests sipped champagne and Kentucky Governor "Happy" Chandler declared Man o' War was now old enough to vote.

Big Red was the state's Number No. 1 tourist attraction, no small economic boost. Over 25 years, the World Almanac estimated, more than 1.5 million people came to Faraway Farm to see him.

Man o' War died on November 1, 1947 at 1:15 p.m. EST at the age of 30 years and seven months, after suffering a heart attack, his fourth. His best friend, Will Harbut, had passed away 29 days earlier.

Big Red's first heart attack occurred after serving his first mare of the 1943 season. His doctor, Charles E. "Charlie" Hagyard, known as the "society doctor of horsedom," was called immediately. Hagyard, who also took care of all of the elite stock at Idle Hour and Calumet, made it clear: "You have the choice of continuing his stud activities and gaining for the world a few more of his sons and daughters, and in a short time losing him; or, if he is retired and lives a quiet life in semi-seclusion, he may have many more years ahead of him. My advice: retire him." And that is exactly what Samuel Riddle did.

What is ironic, as well as telling of a true professional, is that Charlie Hagyard had tried for years to receive a season to Man o' War and was courteously denied. In 1943, his mare Rude Awakening was finally granted a booking to the great stallion and it was the good doctor's own recommendation that effectively eliminated his last chance of getting such a foal. Moreover, the Kentucky Oaks-placed Rude Awakening would have been the first daughter of Red's one-time conqueror Upset to be bred to him. Interestingly, her foal that year, the filly Roused, became the dam of Santa Anita Derby winner Rough 'N Tumble, sire of the great Dr. Fager.

Man o' War was the first horse to have a formal funeral. His embalmed body lay in state in an oak casket lined in the yellow and black colors of Glen Riddle Stable. Over 2,000 people attended the funeral which was broadcast over radio throughout the nation.

152

More than 2,000 people attended Man o' War's funeral at Faraway Farm, which was broadcast nationally over radio and then covered in the newsreels. The great stallion was the first horse ever to be embalmed, and the first, for that matter, to have a formal funeral. For a day before the service, Big Red's body lay in state in his oak casket, lined with the yellow and black colors of Glen Riddle Stable. Before the huge box was lowered into the ground, buglers from the Man o' War Post of the American Legion sounded the clear, sad notes of taps.

Red's remains were ultimately moved, for security reasons, about 10 miles west to the Kentucky Horse Park. As a concession to the expressed wishes of Samuel Riddle that no admission fees be charged visitors to Man o' War's grave, the park's premiere tourist attraction was installed outside its gates. The park's Man o' War statue is a 20 hands high bronze colossus commissioned by Riddle and crafted by eminent animal sculptor Herbert Haseltine. It is a most worthy and lasting tribute.

Figure 11

TAIL MALE DESCENDANTS OF MAN O' WAR IN RACING'S HALL OF FAME
Hall of Famers in **BOLD CAPITALS**

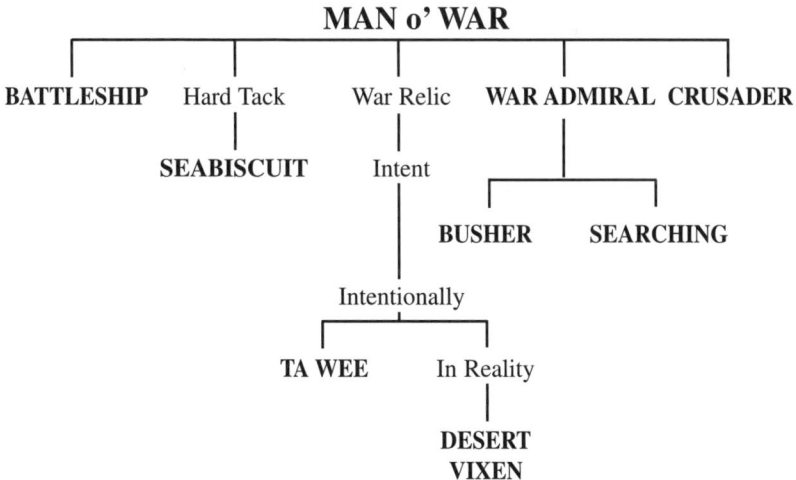

MAN o' WAR

BATTLESHIP	Hard Tack	War Relic	**WAR ADMIRAL**	**CRUSADER**
	SEABISCUIT	Intent		

BUSHER   SEARCHING

Intentionally

TA WEE   In Reality

DESERT
VIXEN

Every time a major poll among writers and historians was taken as to who the best American racehorse is, Man o' War prevails. In the Associated Press Mid-Century poll, he received 305 of 388 votes. Citation, in second, had only 38. As the 20th century came to a close, the AP and *The Blood-Horse* both had Man o' War ranked Number 1, greater even than Secretariat – the second "Big Red."

There are, of course, no simple formulas to measure or rank Man o' War's influence on the breed. The most lucid statistical evidence of Big Red's enrichment of the Thoroughbred gene pool comes from an article entitled "Time, theory, superstition, and science" by John P. Sparkman, William H. Oldknow and David B. Foye (*Thoroughbred Times*, April 18, 1994). In it, the authors found that the prevalence and concentration of Man o' War's blood was significantly higher in an elite population made up of recent multiple Grade or Group 1 winners than in a random control group comprised of mostly average racehorses.

The Man o' War sire line has, for the most part, remained an American institution with only one important instance of successful migration. Much of the reason for this is that for more than a quarter of a century, his blood was prohibited as breeding stock in countries abiding by the *English Stud Book* and the Jersey Act of 1913. Man o' War, it seems, suffered from the same "impurities" in his ancestry as most of his American contemporaries: the blood of Lexington, broodmare sire of Spendthrift, Red's paternal great grandsire. The principal victims of the measure were the English and Irish breeders, for during the Jersey Act's 36-year enforcement they essentially cut themselves off from some of the world's most potent bloodlines including, of course, the line of Man o' War.

In the years immediately following World War II, the case for rescinding the Jersey Act became increasingly strong. It reached a breaking point in 1948 when My Babu won the Two Thousand Guineas and Black Tarquin won the St. Leger, both ineligible from the *English Stud Book* from the "stain" of Lexington. Black Tarquin's granddam, in fact, was the good Man o' War mare Valkyr. It was also now clear to most that the "impurities" which had formed the original bone of contention had become so remote as to possess very little significance and, thus, the statute was repealed in 1949.

Soon thereafter, in 1951, the Man o' War male line made its one and only inroad into Europe with the importation of War Relic's son Relic to France. There, Relic became a very successful sire with an emphasis on speed. His daughters, the full sisters Texana and Texanita, won three runnings of the Prix de l'Abbaye de Longchamp while his son Buisson Ardent captured the French Two Thousand Guineas. Another son, Olden Times, was imported "in utero" to the U.S., where he became an important winner and sire. A good number of Relic's other sons, in fact, spread his male line throughout the world with distinction for several decades, but very little has been heard from this branch since the early 1990s, and it does appear that its flame as a tail-male line has just about gone out.

Figure 12

THE SURVIVING BRANCHES OF THE MAN O' WAR SIRE LINE

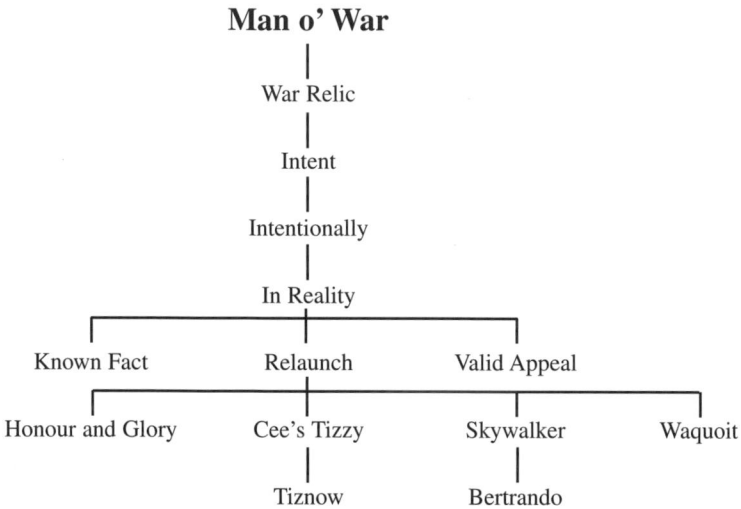

Man o' War
|
War Relic
|
Intent
|
Intentionally
|
In Reality
|
Known Fact — Relaunch — Valid Appeal

Honour and Glory — Cee's Tizzy — Skywalker — Waquoit
|
Tiznow — Bertrando

The Thoroughbred's diversity of male lines has been declining steadily over the past 40 years and coincides with the increasing dominance of the Phalaris sire line, what breeding theorist Franco Varola referred to as the "Phalaris revolution." The once thriving male lines of Broomstick, Sir Gallahad III, Bull Lea and many others have, indeed, all vanished.

As a result, there are, at present, only a handful of viable "non-Phalaris" sire lines still left in the U.S. One of these is the line of Man o' War through his son War Relic, sire of Intent, the sire of Intentionally, whose son In Reality still enjoys several succeeding branches (Figure 12).

Intent's pedigree appears in Chapter 7. His best son, Futurity Stakes winner Intentionally, was also bred by Harry Isaacs. In 1959 at age three, he was named champion sprinter. Intentionally's pedigree followed a similar pattern to War Relic's champion son Battlefield who was out of a Display mare, while Intentionally was from a daughter of Display's best son Discovery, creating inbreeding to Fair Play 4x4 and the family of Fair Play (Fairy Gold 5x5x5).

Intentionally was eventually sold by Isaacs to Tartan Farms in Florida where he became a foundation stallion after his best son, In Reality, expanded the breadth of the line with a number of good sons at stud.

In Reality's pedigree represented a second consecutive generation of close inbreeding to the tail-male line as his granddam Iltis was a daughter of War Relic, creating his 3x3 duplication. In all, In Reality carried three strains of Fair Play and two more of his half-brother Friar Rock.

In Reality was an outstanding stallion. Remarkably, a close look at the pedigrees of his progeny reveals that much his success came when he was bred to mares carrying the blood of Equipoise. This, not coincidentally, created inbreeding to the families of his sire, Intentionally, and grandsire, Intent.

Intentionally's fourth dam, Balancoire, was Equipoise's granddam, while Intent's fourth dam, Cherokee Rose II, was a full sister to Equipoise's sire, Pennant. Even though Equipoise appeared in the pedigrees of less than 15 percent of the mares In Reality was bred to, he appeared in the large majority of that stallion's best get including Racing Hall of Fame filly Desert Vixen, as well as the important sires Known Fact, Believe It, Valid Appeal and his best son at stud, Relaunch.

Another interesting aspect to In Reality's influence is his disproportionately high appearance in the pedigrees of runners who do particularly well on off tracks. There is also an increasing number of wet track winners carrying more than one of his strains. Right now,

In Reality is probably the most important ingredient in the pedigree of the contemporary American "mudlark."

Of course, Man o' War relished any going. His offspring Crusader and Siren loved an off track while others such as War Admiral and his three-quarters brother War Glory certainly did not.

In recent years, Big Red's most celebrated tail-male descendant is his seventh generation scion Tiznow (by Cee's Tizzy, by Relaunch). Bred in California, he was 2000 Horse of the Year and is the only two-time winner of the Breeders' Cup Classic (G1).

Early impressions that the tall, gangly yearling Man o' War looked like a good hunter prospect turned out to be prophetic as his blood became a primary source of top steeplechasers for generations to come.

Man o' War's influence over the jumps began to truly manifest itself during the mid-1930s, starting with 1936 American steeplechase champion Bushranger who was out of a Man o' War mare and trained by Sam Riddle's old college pal and racing partner John Howard Lewis. In all, Lewis trained 14 champions, including Fairmount (Fair Play-Sunflower by Rock Sand), one of the best from the 1920s. Fairmount, Bushranger and J. Howard Lewis have all been inducted into the Racing Hall of Fame.

In 1938, Man o' War's 11-year-old son Battleship, another Hall of Famer, became the first American-bred and owned horse to win the English Grand National at Aintree. A year later, Red's son Blockade (ch. g., 1929, out of Rock Emerald by Trap Rock) won the first of three consecutive runnings of the grueling Maryland Hunt Cup, taking seven seconds off course time in the process.

Man o' War's son Annapolis, himself a good winner over the jumps, went on to become a superior sire of steeplechasers getting four American champions: Rouge Dragon in 1944, Mercator in 1945, The Mast in 1947 and Benguala in 1960.

Battleship also became an excellent sire of steeplechasers with two American champions: War Battle in 1947 and Shipboard in 1956. Moreover, Shipboard was out of an Annapolis mare and, thus, was closely inbred (2x3) to Man o' War. Three time Eclipse winner Neji (1955, 1957, 1958) was also out of an Annapolis mare.

Throughout the balance of the century, Man o' War's influence among top jumpers remained strong, culminating in the final decade with Lonesome Glory, the only American steeplechase horse to ever win five Eclipse Awards (1992-93, 1995, 1997, 1999) and the first to earn more than $1 million.

Lonesome Glory, by Transworld, was owned by Kay Jeffords and bred by her husband, Walter M. Jeffords Jr. He also bred the Hall of Famer's dam, the unraced Green Dancer mare Stronghold, whose pedigree featured 5x2 inbreeding to Blue Denim in Formula One fashion (Stronghold's granddam Blue Denim was also the fourth dam of Green Dancer). Initiating the legacy was Blue Denim herself, a granddaughter of Man o' War, who was bred by Walter M. Jeffords Sr. almost four decades earlier. Lonesome Glory was raised in Kentucky at Shandon Farm by Harry Scott, the son of Faraway Farm's long-time manager Harrie B. Scott.

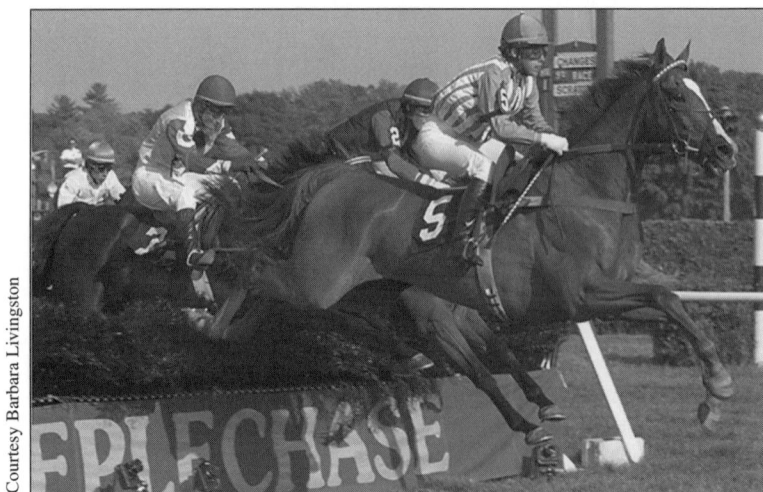

Courtesy Barbara Livingston

Lonesome Glory was inducted into the National Museum of Racing's Hall of Fame in 2005. Campaigned by Mrs. Walter Jeffords Jr., Lonesome Glory was a five-time winner of the Eclipse Award as the nation's top horse over fences, and was the first steeplechase champion to win over $1 million.

One of the more interesting and historically under-acknowledged characters in the Man o' War story is Englishman William Allison who was integral in getting Big Red off to his powerful start at stud with the

European broodmares he selected. Allison, always a controversial figure, seems to have been remembered much more for his banter than his actions, which if added up would constitute an incomparable level of influence and achievement in the Thoroughbred world.

Trained as a barrister, Allison entered the sporting world with a fierce, political style that he applied freely to his turf writing. Sometimes, he simply devoted space in his columns to his unadulterated brand of politics. As "Special Commissioner" for *The Sportsman*, he engaged in many journalistic skirmishes with his counterpart, the esteemed J.B. Robertson, known as "Mankato" from *The Sporting Chronicle* and *The Bloodstock Breeders' Review*.

From *Memories of Men and Horses*

William Allison

Allison's published articles were also often compromised by his chronic habit of "plugging" whatever business interests he was currently involved in, particularly any stallion with which he was connected. This was generally accepted with "amused toleration." Then, of course, there was Allison's championing of Lowe's "figure system," thought of in some circles as the harbinger of the subsequent and oppressive Jersey Act.

What hardly ever seems to get mentioned is that William Allison's one-man bloodstock outfit, The International Horse Agency and Exchange Ltd., was involved in much of the development of all three great American sire lines of the early 20th century: Domino, Ben Brush and Fair Play!

Allison purchased the mares for Keene and Daingerfield at Castleton that produced or founded the families of many of the most influential racers and sires of that era including Domino's grandson Peter Pan and his sons Pennant and Black Toney, as well as Sweep and Broomstick, the two primary sons of Ben Brush. Allison sent August Belmont II both the dam of Fair Play and the granddam of Man o' War. For Riddle, Allison picked up the third dam of War Admiral, Man o' War's best son.

In two other key transactions during his career, William Allison was responsible for forming the syndicate that returned influential sire Tracery to England in 1923, after Major Belmont sold him to Argentine interests in 1920. Even more important was Allison's earlier transfer to England of Trenton, a son of Musket that he imported from Australia in 1896. Trenton would leave an indelible mark on the English racehorse as the sire of Rosaline, dam of Oaks winner Rosedrop who produced Triple Crown winner Gainsborough, who, in turn, sired the great Hyperion.

Allison's promotion of the "figure system" did, in fact, prove to be a valuable contribution since, if nothing else, the method for female family classification it constructed has been used ever since. Lowe and Allison's numbering system did for Thoroughbred family identification what the zip code did for mail delivery.

With all of this, one finds relatively very little reference to William Allison in the appropriate racing literature since his death in 1925. It is quite odd how both English and American histories seem to have written out much of his tremendous impact on the evolution of the breed.

After Mrs. Elizabeth Riddle's death in 1942, Riddle, now in his 80s, remained a frequent and enthusiastic participant at the metropolitan courses. He was by most accounts a gregarious sort who counted among his many previous acquaintances the reticent President Calvin Coolidge with whom Riddle mused, "I used to talk horses."

Besides all of his influence as a breeder, Riddle's greatest achievement in racing is, simply, that no other American Thoroughbred owner has ever campaigned a colt as good as Man o' War – or two colts as good as Man o' War and War Admiral.

Samuel Riddle died on January 8, 1951, at his home and birthplace in Glen Riddle, Pennsylvania. The 89-year-old was seriously ill for about two weeks. He was buried in his family's plot, beneath a 10-foot-high obelisk in the cemetery of Media's Middletown Presbyterian Church.

Glen Riddle racing stable was dispersed at Hialeah the following month. Fourteen horses in training sold for $152,300. Eighteen others went for $41,886. The highest price was paid for Shy Bim, a three-year-old daughter of Bimelech, fetching $27,500. Shy Bim's daughter Shy Dancer (by Bolero) would, in time, become an important matriarch, forging the family of champion filly Heavenly Cause and Breeders' Cup Mile winner Opening Verse. Most of the remaining Glen Riddle broodmares were eventually purchased by California horseman Rex Ellsworth, best known as the owner and breeder of Swaps.

The bulk of the Riddle estate was left to a fund for the establishment of a non-profit, full-facility hospital in Media, Pennsylvania. The Riddle portion of Faraway Farm continued in operation for several more years with the proceeds from the sale of yearlings and the stud fees of War Admiral and War Relic also contributed to this fund. In February 1963, Riddle Memorial Hospital was finally opened, later to be followed by the adjoining Riddle Village, a non-profit retirement community, all on 72 acres along Route 1 across from Granite Run Mall, where Glen Riddle once stood. Most of the village's residential lanes are named after the horses that carried Glen Riddle's colors to victory. When Sam Riddle died, this area was still mostly rural, but Philadelphia and its suburbs have grown far past Media since then. The master of Glen Riddle surely would have been proud that Riddle Memorial's Intensive Care Unit was recently recognized as one of the finest in the nation.

While the Jeffords never raced a horse as good as Man o' War, or even War Admiral, they did campaign more champions than their uncle, enjoying periods of tremendous success along the way.

Jeffords, always deeply concerned with the problems of turf administration and the conduct of racing, had a long and distinguished record of service in the Thoroughbred industry. Elected to the Jockey Club in 1925, he served on its Board of Stewards from 1941 to 1949. Jeffords was also one of the driving forces in the creation of the Grayson Foundation in 1940, providing a perpetual source of funding for research into equine health and safety. He was its president from 1947 to 1952.

Jeffords was guest of honor at the Thoroughbred Club of America's annual dinner in 1950. He lent his support to the establishment of the National Museum of Racing in 1951, becoming its second president in 1954. The Jeffords donated many fine pieces to the museum. Jeffords was an ardent student of turf literature and history and an avid collector of racing art. He actively searched out the works of a number of artists including Edward Troye and his uncle's old pal Henry Stull. The Jeffords also enjoyed putting together one of the finest collections of Early American silver and furniture in the world.

Walter M. Jeffords died on September 28, 1960. Mrs. Sarah Jeffords continued to breed and race horses until her death in 1966. At that point, Walter M. "Jeff" Jeffords, Jr. took up the calling and prior to his own death in 1990, extended the family legacy by breeding 10 more stakes winners, including the champions Faraway Son and Lonesome Glory. As a tribute to a great horse and a great racing family, a statue of Lonesome Glory now enriches the Racing Museum's grounds at Saratoga Springs across from the historic racecourse.

The Jeffords' pack of Penn-Marydel hounds established originally by Riddle now live on Iron Mountain Ranch in Colorado where their primary purpose is to chase the over-abundant coyotes from the nesting areas of endangered ground nesting birds.

After Riddle's death, Glen Riddle Farm on Maryland's Eastern Shore continued as a training center for the Jeffords family. In April 1969, however, a fire destroyed the mansion, exactly 100 years after it was built. The interior, filled with priceless antique furniture and racing memorabilia, was completely gutted as the firetrucks ran out of water and had to pump it from a pond several hundred yards away. The farm began a slow slide toward decay after that. In recent years, this land has been marked for redevelopment. Centex Homes is the lead developer in transforming Glen Riddle into GlenRiddle, a gated community of 650 homes that will include a 96-slip marina on Herring Creek providing access to the Atlantic Ocean. There will also be the "Man o' War" and "War Admiral" championship golf courses. Plans are for the original stallion barn – which featured three cupolas and 24 oversized stalls – to be preserved and converted into the golf clubhouse. The project is expected to be completed by 2006.

Gone are the days each annum when the yearlings arrived from Kentucky at the Maryland training center, one of the great local interests for the little County of Worcester. The curious would gather along the railroad siding near Holly Grove Road to watch the yearlings led off the train and down the path to the farm, many hoping to get a first glance at the next great champion.

Riddle's portion of Faraway Farm was not sold by his estate until 1958, while the Jeffords' share stayed in the family until recently. Within the last year, restorative improvements to the original stallion barn were completed which included the affixing of brass nameplates of each stallion to the appropriate stalls.

In 1958, War Admiral, War Relic and several others were moved from Faraway to Preston Madden's Hamburg Place, the legendary Lexington farm where Preston's grandfather, "The Wizard of the Turf," John E. Madden bred five Kentucky Derby winners [Old Rosebud (1911), Sir Barton (1916), Paul Jones (1917), Zev (1920) and Flying Ebony (1922)]. The elder Madden had, of course, helped ease Riddle and Jeffords into major league racing more than four decades earlier, selling them some of their first stakes winners as well as stakes producing mares, including the dam of Crusader.

The Man o' War story came full circle when the last War Admiral foal bred by Preston Madden was the 1960 filly Belthazar, out of the old Colonel Bradley mare Blinking Owl. Unraced herself, she became the granddam of 1987 Kentucky Derby winner Alysheba, an amazing sixth Derby winner bred at Hamburg Place. Alysheba retired at the end of the 1988 season, like his great-great grandsire Man o' War before him, as America's richest racehorse ($6,679,242).

The establishment of Glen Riddle Farm, in the mid-1910s, as a state-of-the-art Thoroughbred training center served notice that Riddle was committed to excel while competing at the highest levels.

Over the course of the next several years, Riddle and his nephew, Jeffords, set the foundations for their own racing and breeding dynasties by simply following the same avenues to success as the three greatest owner-breeders of the period: Madden, Belmont and Whitney. This meant acquiring the best of their available bloodlines and expertise, and then applying similar breeding and business strategies.

Riddle and Jeffords graduated from moderate to black type winners when they began buying young stock from John E. Madden, the premiere commercial breeder of his day. It was a relationship which continued into the 1920s with the purchase of some of Man o' War's most important mares.

Riddle's admiration of the Belmont empire was first manifested with the hiring of trainer Louis Feustel. It was the first in a series of steps leading to the acquisition and racing exploits of Man o' War, the ultimate Belmont homebred. When it came to selecting European broodmare prospects for Big Red, Riddle and Jeffords turned to William Allison who previously had brought Belmont's Nursery Stud to new heights with the importations of Fairy Gold and Merry Token.

The Riddle and Jeffords camps both maintained August Belmont's penchant for contests of stamina over speed, with a particularly keen eye on New York's classic distance events.

The third great horseman emulated by Riddle and Jeffords was Harry Payne Whitney, whose Thoroughbred empire consisted of the best blood from the stud of his father, William Collins Whitney, as well as the rich stock he acquired from the dispersal of J. R. Keene's Castleton Stud. Castleton's fortunes were sparked by the broodmare importations of the omnipresent English agent, Mr. Allison. Their high-yield matings were arranged by Major Foxhall Daingerfield whose accomplished daughter Miss Elizabeth was brought in to serve as Faraway Farm's first manager.

The Jeffords exhibited their regard for Whitney blood when they spent a record amount to acquire Golden Broom, the very close relative of his Derby heroine Regret. H. P. Whitney-bred mares later served as important producers at Faraway for both Riddle and Jeffords. When Cornelius Vanderbilt Whitney followed in his father's footsteps, the exchange of prime Thoroughbred blood with Faraway expanded even further.

By the early 1930s, Faraway Farm had Man o' War, as well as four of his best sons, at stud. Since access to Big Red's services was limited, the farm benefited from its ability to offer many of the best alternatives to breeders specifically seeking Man o' War blood. It was a strategy employed by H. P. Whitney whose 1928 studbook listed among its stallions Broomstick, five of his best sons and two more of his prominent male-line grandsons. Creating speculative monopolies was an approach to business Whitney's father, W. C., practiced with distinction as he rose in wealth and prestige during the late 19th century. The H. P. Whitney Stud and Faraway Farm maintained similar positions with the blood of their foundation stallions, Broomstick and Man o' War.

Another important similarity between Faraway Farm and the H. P. Whitney Stud was the common appearance of female family inbreeding patterns within the pedigrees of their foals, particularly along the tail-male line of their foundation sires. Many of the best Whitney-breds had pedigrees demonstrating inbreeding to the families of Domino and Broomstick, his sire Ben Brush, as well as his great grandsire Bonnie Scotland. Many of the mares bred to Man o' War contributed complementary strains from the tribes of Fair Play, Hastings and Spendthrift.

The final caveat from all of this is that a remarkable number of top American runners in recent years have featured pedigrees which demonstrate duplications of some of the potent affinities that were described. For example, multiple strains of the War Admiral/La Troienne cross can be observed in three of the last 11 Kentucky Derby winners' pedigrees, Sea Hero in 1993 (Busanda & Searching 3x3), Silver Charm in 1997 (Busanda & Striking 3x4) and Smarty Jones in 2004 (Searching & Striking 6x5).

Table 10 COMPARING THE SIRE INFLUENCE OF AMERICA'S TOP RACEHORSES OF THE TWENTIETH CENTURY

		Year Foaled	SWs	% SWs	# HoF	Sire Line Viability
1	MAN O' WAR	1917	64	17%	3	strong
2	SECRETARIAT	1970	57	9%	1	weak
3	CITATION	1945	12	4%	1	extinct
4	KELSO	1957	–	–	–	gelding
5	COUNT FLEET	1940	37	9%	0	extinct
6	DR. FAGER	1964	35	14%	0	extinct
7	NATIVE DANCER	1950	44	14%	0	very strong
8	FOREGO	1970	–	–	–	gelding
9	SEATTLE SLEW	1974	110	11%	2	very strong
10	SPECTACULAR BID	1976	44	6%	0	weak
11	TOM FOOL	1949	36	13%	2	fair
12	AFFIRMED	1975	85	10%	1	weak
13	WAR ADMIRAL	1934	40	11%	2	extinct
14	BUCKPASSER	1963	35	11%	1	fair
15	COLIN	1905	11	14%	0	fair
16	DAMASCUS	1964	71	10%	0	strong
17	ROUND TABLE	1954	83	21%	0	weak
18	CIGAR	1990	–	–	–	sterile
19	BOLD RULER	1954	82	23%	2	very strong
20	SWAPS	1952	35	8%	1	extinct

HoF = number of offspring in Racing's Hall of Fame
Rankings were determined by a recognized panel assembled by *The Blood-Horse* magazine in 1999

Assuming Man o' War was not expected to halt the "avalanche of Phalaris," then it is probably a tribute to his potency that his male line is still even viable, let alone healthy, seven or eight generations later.

If the Man o' War sire line is to survive in the future it will do so by continuing in its ability to issue good winners, not by any altruistic desire to perpetuate it. And, if history continues to be our best guide, the most favorable pathways will involve the creation of female family inbreeding patterns.

Finally, if analysis of Man o' War's stud career had shown that the quality of his offspring was dependent on the racing class of his mares, irrespective of other key variables, then a case could have been mounted in support of Big Red's missed opportunities and, perhaps, even mismanagement. But that was never the case.

Was Riddle incredibly lucky to get Man o' War? Of course.

Did he know what to do with him once he got him? Absolutely.

Sometimes that can drive other people crazy.

Courtesy of University of Kentucky Libraries

In Riddle's obituary in the January 13, 1951 issue of *The Thoroughbred Record*, Frank Talmadge Phelps wrote, "Fortune is at times capricious, slighting the deserving and favoring those who do not seem to merit her smiles, but she made no mistake when she linked the fates of Man o' War with Sam Riddle.

"He was a man worthy of 'de mostest hoss.'"

Table 11   STAKES WINNERS BRED BY SAMUEL D. RIDDLE

Stakes Winner	sire - dam	broodmare sire	earnings	family #	racing distinctions
LONG POINT b. g. 1921	Ballot-Ursula Emma	Broomstick	$44,835	A1	Henderson H., etc.
AMERICAN FLAG ch. c. 1922	Man o' War-Lady Comfey	Roi Herode	$82,725	7	Champion 3 YO Colt, Belmont S.
GUN BOAT ch. g. 1922	Man o' War-Star Fancy	Star Shoot	$26,500	4-m	Woodbine Steeplechase H., etc.
MAID AT ARMS ch. f. 1922	Man o' War-Trasher	Trap Rock	$29,305	3-n	co-Champion 3 YO F, Alabama S
CORVETTE ch. f. 1923	Man o' War-Batanoea	Roi Herode	$12,225	4-n	Gazelle S., 2nd Manor H., Test S.
CRUSADER ch. c. 1923	Man o' War-Star Fancy	Star Shoot	$203,261	4-m	1926 Horse of Year, Belmont S.
TAPS ch. f. 1923	Man o' War-Shady	Broomstick	$24,500	16	Matron S., Schuylerville S.
FRIAR'S CARSE ch. f. 1923	Friar Rock-Problem	Superman	$20,225	1-o	Champion 2 YO filly; Fashion S.
FULL DRESS blk. c. 1927	Man o' War-Shady	Broomstick	$8,820	16	Hermis H.
FLEET FLAG ch. g. 1928	Man o' War-Lady Comfey	Roi Herode	$14,260	7	Amsterdam Claiming S.
GREAT GUN ch. g. 1928	American Flag-Scribble	Ultimus	$7,860	6	Maturity Stakes
SEA FOX ch. g. 1928	Man o' War-Trasher	Trap Rock	$24,465	3-n	Hampton Cup H., Pingree H.
WAR HERO b. c. 1929	Man o' War-Whetstone	Sweep	$38,361	1-j	Travers Stakes, Saratoga Cup
WAR PLANE ch. g. 1929	American Flag-Milky Way	Star Shoot	$21,777	9	General Beauregard Cl. S.
SPEED BOAT ch. f. 1930	Man o' War-Friar's Carse	Friar Rock	$6,145	1-o	Adirondack H., Test S.
WAR GLORY ch. c. 1930	Man o' War-Annette K.	Harry of Hereford	$55,050	11-g	Lawrence Realization S., etc.
ARSON b. f. 1931	Big Blaze-Shady	Broomstick	$17,715	16	Golden Gate Bridge Handicap
ARMY GAME ch. f. 1932	Bright Knight-Maid At Arms	Man o' War	$8,825	3-n	Quebec Derby
GOLD FOAM ch. c. 1932	Golden Broom-Assembly	Man o' War	$21,235	6-b	Travers S., Seneca Cl.

Stakes Winner	sire - dam	broodmare sire	earnings	family #	racing distinctions
MCCARTHY ch. g. 1932	Star Master-Confusion	Friar Rock	$20,500	11	Louisiana Derby, Polo Park H.
SHIP EXECUTIVE ch. g. 1932	Man o' War-Lady Comfey	Roi Herode	$14,000	7	Meadow Brook Stp. H., etc.
STAR SHADOW dkb/br. g. 1932	Man o' War-Shady	Broomstick	$39,310	16	World's Fair H., Arlington Fall H.
WAR ADMIRAL br. c. 1934	Man o' War-Brushup	Sweep	$273,240	11-g	Triple Crown, 1937 Horse of Year
MANDINGHAM ch. g. 1934	The Satrap-Float	Man o' War	$18,875	5-i	Georgetown & Glendale Stp. H.
MANIE O'HARA gr. f. 1935	The Satrap-Boadicea	Man o' War	$20,922	3	Marquette H., Steger H., etc.
U-BOAT blk. f. 1935	Man o' War-Artifice	Light Brigade	$17,460	4-m	Worcester H.
GET OFF br. c. 1936	American Flag-On Her Toes	High Time	$41,740	2-o	Palm Beach Handicap
BATTLE COLORS ch. g. 1938	Man o' War-Beaugingham	Sun Briar	$20,925	4-p	Will Rogers Handicap
LEVEL BEST ch. f. 1938	Equipoise-Speed Boat	Man o' War	$64,230	1-o	Champion 2 YO Filly; CCA Oaks
WAR HAZARD ch. f. 1938	Man o' War-Artifice	Light Brigade	$20,315	4-m	Alabama S.
WAR RELIC ch. c. 1938	Man o' War-Friar's Carse	Friar Rock	$89,495	1-o	Massachusetts H., Kenner S.
DENSE PATH ch. f. 1939	Blackwood-Harmonessa	Bull Dog	$24,590	10	Rockingham Park Handicap
SOLDIER SONG b. g. 1939	Man o' War-Song	Royal Minstrel	$39,230	3-n	Laurel Stakes
*THUMBS UP b. c. 1939	Blenheim II-Gas Bag	Man o' War	$249,290	2-d	Santa Anita H., San Pasqual H.
BLUE SWORDS b. c. 1940	Blue Larkspur-Flaming Swords	Man o' War	$58,065	7	Remsen H., 2nd Kentucky Derby
NO WRINKLES ch. c. 1940	Wise Counsellor-Crows Feet	Man o' War	$68,590	6	Bay Meadows H., New Year's H.
STRATEGIC br. g. 1940	American Flag-Artifice	Light Brigade	$41,725	4-m	Edgemere H., Survivor S.
DIRECTOR J.E. br. c. 1941	Sickle-Dead Reckoning	Man o' War	$52,397	7-c	Jennings H., Richard Johnson S.
FLOAT ME br. g. 1941	Menow-Float	Man o' War	$72,055	5-i	Au Revoir H. (3X), Governor's H.
RODNEY STONE b. c. 1941	Bull Dog-War Lassie	Man o' War	$31,230	2-d	Sanford S., Albany H.
*RAMPART blk. f. 1942	Trace Call-Boat	Man o' War	$190,840	14-f	Gulfstream Park H., Olympic H.
WAR TROPHY blk. g. 1942	Trace Call-Racing Colors	Man o' War	$136,685	2-n	Riggs H., Rhode Island H., etc.
WAR KILT ch. f. 1943	Man o' War-Friar's Carse	Friar Rock	$13,845	1-o	Demoiselle Stakes

*THE SHAKER b. g. 1943	Roman-War Jitters	Man o' War	$79,572	2-o	Hollywood Premiere H., etc.
SYMPOSIUM gr. g. 1947	War Relic-Betsy Ross	Mahmoud	$33,000	9-f	Camden Handicap
MR. WHY b. g. 1948	Onslaught II-Flying Goddess	Jas. T. Clark	$10,235	19	Bird Catcher S., Salisbury Juv. S
BRUSH BURN b. g. 1949	Bernborough-My Brush	Menow	$211,187	11-g	Meadowland H., Grassland H.
WAR AGE br. c. 1949	War Relic-Ellendale	Bimelech	$99,065	1-o	Maryland Sprint Handicap
BRADLEY br. c. 1950	Bimelech-Our Colors	Man o' War	$104,445	11-g	Sanford S., Great American S.
FORT SALONGA gr. c. 1950	Mahmoud-Fortify	Case Ace	$33,700	12-b	Juvenile S., William Penn S.
**RED HANNIGAN ch. c. 1951	Heliopolis-War Damsel	Man o' War	$169,187	20-a	Carter H., Bay Shore H., etc.
**ADMIRAL VEE ch. c. 1952	War Admiral-Yankee Flirt	Blenheim II	$315,795	4-m	Saratoga H., Paumonok H., etc.
**BREAUX dkb/br. c. 1957	War Admiral-Boot All	Our Boots	$35,097	1-1	Youthful S., Cincinnati Trophy
**WAR COUNCIL b. c. 1958	Somali II-Warpatia	War Admiral	$174,092	13-c	Chicago H., South. Maryland H.

*   bred by Riddle & Harrie B. Scott

** Samuel D. Riddle Estate

Table 12 STAKES WINNERS OWNED BUT NOT BRED BY SAMUEL RIDDLE & WALTER JEFFORDS

Stakes Winner	sire - dam - broodmare sire	earnings	breeder	owner	racing distinctions
SWARTHMORE ch. c. 1884	Stampede-Blossom by Pat Malloy	unknown	JH Lewis	R	Kenner Stakes
YANKEE WITCH b. f. 1914	Ogden-Event by Adam	unknown	Madden	R	Spinaway Stakes, Rosedale S.
STAR HAMPTON ch. c. 1916	Star Shoot-Doro. Hampton by Royal Hampton	$8,038	Madden	J	Albany H., Colorado S.
ROUTLEDGE ch. c. 1916	Toddington-Understudy by Star Ruby	$20,465	McDowell	J	Adirondack Handicap
MAN O' WAR ch. c. 1917	Fair Play-Mahubah by Rock Sand	$249,465	Belmont II	R	**Horse of the Century**
GOLDEN BROOM ch. c. 1917	Sweeper-Zuna by Hamburg	$10,050	H Duryea	J	Saratoga Special
KINNOUL ch. c. 1917	Peter Quince-Lychee Nut by Sir Modred	$8,998	L. Combs	J	Albany H., Pimlico Nursery S.
DINNA CARE ch. c. 1917	Superman-Dinawick by Childwick	$22,018	HT Oxnard	R	Saranac H., Expectation H., etc.
OCEANIC blk/br. c. 1919	The Finn-Veuve Clicquot by McGee	$32,962	Madden	R	Washington H., Pim. Autumn H.
TEN MINUTES blk. c. 1920	Hourless-Pamphyle by Robert Le Diable	$10,105	Xalapa	R	Expectation Handicap
BIG BLAZE b. c. 1921	Campfire-Queen of the Hills by Kt of Thistle	$81,863	Potter	R	Washington H., Manor H.
WHETSTONE b. f. 1921	Sweep-Keystone by Marajax	$21,400	HmyarStd	R	Ladies Handicap, Brookdale H.

Table 13   STAKES WINNERS BRED BY MR. & MRS. WALTER M. JEFFORDS SR.

Stakes Winner	sire - dam	broodmare sire	earnings	family #	racing distinctions
COCKNEY ch. g. 1921	Great Britain-L'Avenir	Rabelais	$22,705	4-r	Pimlico Homebred Stakes
DIOGENES ch. g. 1921	Ballot-Smoky Lamp	Plaudit	$49,975	12-b	Hopeful Stakes
BY HISSELF br. c. 1922	Man o' War-Colette	Collar	$21,175	20	Ardsley H., Bayview H., etc.
FLORENCE NIGHTINGALE br. f. 1922	Man o' War-The Nurse	Yankee	$18,650	23-b	co-Champion 3 YO Filly
EDITH CAVELL b. f. 1923	Man o' War-The Nurse	Yankee	$69,329	23-b	co-Champion 3 YO Filly
MARS ch. c. 1923	Man o' War-Christmas Star	Star Shoot	$128,786	2-c	Travers Stakes, Dixie H., etc.
*SCAPA FLOW b. c. 1924	Man o' War-Florence Webber	Peep O' Day	$93,955	4-m	Champion 2 YO Colt, Futurity S.
*SON O' BATTLE b. c. 1924	Man o' War-Batanoea	Roi Herode	$27,225	4-n	Toronto Cup H., Ballston H.
*TRITON b. c. 1924	Golden Broom-Bathing Girl	Spearmint	$19,530	11-g	Harford H., Pimlico Nursery S.
BATEAU b. f. 1925	Man o' War-Escuina	Ecouen	$120,760	9-e	co-Champion Filly at 3; Chp at 4
*GOOD AS GOLD b. f. 1927	Golden Broom-Bel Agnes	Ambassador IV	$18,885	16-c	Pimlico Nursery S., Aberdeen S.
*HAMPTONIAN b. g. 1927	Star Hampton-Colette	Collar	$5,935	20	Woodbine Steeplechase H.
IRONCLAD ch. c. 1928	Man o' War-Violet Mahoney	Colin	$6,880	9-b	Jerome H., 2nd Toboggan H.
BOATSWAIN b. c. 1929	Man o' War-Baton	Hainault	$26,650	4-n	Withers S., 3rd Preakness S.
THURSDAY br. g. 1929	Mars-Pretty Day	Ormondale	$40,045	7-a	Riggs H. (2X), Bryan & O'Hara H.
COMMONWEALTH b. g. 1932	Bostonian-Etoile d'Or	Golden Broom	$7,170	2-c	Endurance Handicap
FIRETHORN br. c. 1932	Sun Briar-Baton Rouge	Man o' War	$74,400	4-n	Jockey Club Gold Cup (2X), etc.
BRIGHT AND EARLY b. c. 1933	Golden Broom-Early Vote	Ed Crump	$31,175	21	Old Colony Stakes
GIANT KILLER br. c. 1933	St. Germans-Escadrille	Man o' War	$22,448	9-e	Au Revoir Handicap
INDOMITABLE dkb/br. g. 1933	Man o' War-Violet Mahoney	Colin	$21,640	9-b	W. P. Burch Memorial H.
JEAN BART b. c. 1933	Man o' War-Escuina	Ecouen	$18,940	9-e	Huron H., 3rd Preakness S.
KEARSARGE dkb/br. c. 1933	Man o' War-Baton	Hainault	$5,200	4-n	Miles Standish Handicap

Stakes Winner	sire - dam	broodmare sire	earnings	family #	racing distinctions
WARSPITE ch. g. 1933	Mars-Painted Lady	Golden Broom	$3,625	7-a	Vicmead Highweight Stp. H.
GOLDEN ERA b. g. 1934	Golden Broom-Pretty Day	Ormondale	$19,425	7-a	Pimlico Nursey S., Seneca Cl. S.
MATEY ch. c. 1934	Man o' War-Tavy	St. Germans	$31,750	13-c	Pimlico Futurity
REGAL LILY ch. f. 1934	Man o' War-Regal Lady	Supremus	$23,900	8-g	Alabama S., Gazelle S.
WAND b. f. 1934	Man o' War-Baton	Hainault	$13,525	4-n	Matron Stakes
CREOLE MAID b. f. 1935	Pharamond II-Baton Rouge	Man o' War	$20,950	4-n	CCA Oaks, Adirondack H.
WAR REGALIA ch. f. 1936	Man o' War-Regal Lady	Supremus	$5,260	8-g	Diana Handicap
DAWN ATTACK ch. g. 1938	Mars-Flying Hour	Galetian	$41,870	25	Pawtucket Handicap
FLAUGHT ch. c. 1939	Firethorn-Flying Hour	Galetian	$70,820	25	Tarrytown Cl. S., etc.
GREY WING b. c. 1939	Halcyon-War Grey	Man o' War	$46,810	9-e	Survivor S., Grayson S.
HALBERD ch. c. 1940	Blenheim II-Wand	Man o' War	$9,120	4-n	Saratoga Special Stakes
WESTMINSTER b. g. 1941	Bull Dog-Judy O'Grady	Man o' War	$80,850	16-c	Narragansett Special, etc.
ACE CARD b. f. 1942	Case Ace-Furlough	Man o' War	$30,370	25	Gazelle S., Schuylerville S.
H HOUR ch. g. 1942	Mars-Flying Hour	Galetian	$53,315	25	Amangansett Hurdle H., (2X)
PAVOT br. c. 1942	Case Ace-Coquelicot	Man o' War	$373,365	10-a	Champion Juv. Colt, Belmont S.
TRYMENOW b. c. 1942	Menow-Rambler Rose	Man o' War	$86,320	11-c	Whitney H., Exterminator H., etc.
LOVAT ch. c. 1943	Jamestown-Coquelicot	Man o' War	$40,970	10-a	Choice Stakes
MAHOUT ch. c. 1943	Mahmoud-Ma Minnie	Man o' War	$90,230	4-n	Jerome H., Peter Pan H., etc.
NATCHEZ ch. c. 1943	Jamestown-Creole Maid	Pharamond II	$166,845	4-n	Travers S., 2nd Belmont S., etc.
LOYAL LEGION b. g. 1944	Halcyon-War Grey	Man o' War	$165,435	9-e	Manhattan H., Saratoga H., etc.
SNOW GOOSE gr. f. 1944	Mahmoud-Judy O'Grady	Man o' War	$113,800	16-c	Beldame S., Ladies H., etc.
TAVISTOCK ch. c. 1944	War Admiral-Tavy	St. Germans	$106,930	13-c	Interborough H., 2nd Remsen H.
ADILE ro. f. 1946	Mahmoud-Furlough	Man o' War	$126,825	25	Alabama S., Monmouth Oaks
GREEN BAIZE b. f. 1946	Case Ace-Blue Denim	Blue Larkspur	$29,695	16-c	National Stallion S., Jasmine S.
SAGITTARIUS blk. c. 1946	Teddy's Comet-War Regalia	Man o' War	$119,370	8-g	Jamaica H., New Year's H., etc.

Name	Cross	Sire line	Earnings	Code	Achievements
POST CARD br. c. 1947	Firethorn-Ace Card	Case Ace	$170,942	25	Laurel H., Brandywine H. (2X)
SULEIMAN gr. c. 1947	Mahmoud-Blue Denim	Blue Larkspur	$ 68,677	16-c	Grand Union Hotel S., Capitol H.
KISS ME KATE ch. f. 1948	Count Fleet-Irish Nora	Pharamond II	$196,505	16-c	Champion 3YO Filly; Alabama S.
YILDIZ ch. c. 1948	Mahmoud-Ace Card	Case Ace	$90,475	25	Flamingo Stakes, Brandywine H.
LILY WHITE b. f. 1949	Easton-Magic Lily	Halcyon	$41,100	8-g	Alabama S., 2nd CCA Oaks, etc.
ONE COUNT dkb/br. c. 1949	Count Fleet-Ace Card	Case Ace	$245,225	25	co-Horse of Year & 3 YO champ.
SUBAHDAR b. g. 1950	Alsab-Muti	Mahmoud	$113,400	8-g	Laurel H., Quaker City H., etc.
TAHITI b. c. 1950	Polynesian-Blue Denim	Blue Larkspur	$46,925	16-c	Maryland Sprint H., Dover S.
BLUE PRINCE b. c. 1951	Princequillo-Blue Denim	Blue Larkspur	$3,750	16-c	Zetland Gold Cup, 2nd Ascot GC
MOMUS ch. c. 1952	Natchez-My Rose	Snark	$87,900	10-a	Laurel H., Toronto Cup H.
POLICEMAN DAY b. c. 1952	Challedon-Blue Denim	Blue Larkspur	$69,730	16-c	New York Writers Cup Hcp., etc.
MASUD gr. c. 1953	Mahmoud-War Regalia	Man o' War	$60,480	8-g	Easter H., State of New Mexico H
PIANO JIM b. c. 1955	Bernborough-Blue Denim	Blue Larkspur	$131,109	16-c	Travers Stakes, Laurel H.
MERGANSER blk. c. 1957	Pavot-Snow Goose	Mahmoud	$16,930	16-c	Dover Stakes
*POST EXCHANGE b.c. 1959	Post Card-Artistic	Daumier	$47,605	16	Caesar Rodney Stakes
*RED DOG b.g. 1959	Hafiz-Miss Blue Lea	Bull Lea	$46,549	4-m	Brandywine & Sussex Turf Hcp
**COMMUNIQUE dkb/br. c. 1960	Post Card-Artistic	Daumier	$55,532	16	Hurricane Handicap
**MY CARD dkb/br. f. 1961	My Babu-Ace Card	Case Ace	$98,405	25	Selima Stakes
**ALPS b. f. 1962	Pavot-Alyxia	Alycidon	$61,245	1-e	Chrysanthemum Handicap
**JUANITA b. f. 1962	Decathlon-Pavonia	Pavot	$126,000	25	Delaware Oaks, Betsy Ross H.
**PORTSMOUTH b. c. 1962	Blue Prince-My Rose	Snark	$88,0011	10-a	Maryland H., Sussex Turf H., etc.
**BIRTHDAY CARD b. g. 1964	Post Card-Alyxia	Alycidon	$43,189	1-e	Brandywine Handicap
**LEWISTON b. f. 1964	Rasper II-Mrs. Arris	Pavot	$61,539	16-c	Delaware Oaks
**RED HOOK ch. f. 1964	Royal Sting-Pavonia	Pavot	$16,970	25	Mermaid Stakes
**MOONREINDEER b. g. 1965	Dark Star-Coque Blue	Daumier	$140,030	16-c	Autumn Handicap
**SINGING RAIN b. f. 1965	Sensitivo-Roodles	Princequillo	$212,276	25	Molly Pitcher H., Gallorette H. etc

*   bred by Mr. & Mrs. Walter M. Jeffords Sr.   **   bred by Mrs. Walter M. Jeffords Sr.

INDEX